NORDIC LIGHT

HENRY PLUMMER

NORDIC LIGHT

MODERN SCANDINAVIAN ARCHITECTURE

WITH 513 ILLUSTRATIONS, 441 IN COLOUR

Thames & Hudson

For Juhani Pallasmaa
Nordic friend and kindred spirit,
and for Patty,
in gratitude, for the first forty years.

Henry Plummer is Professor Emeritus of Architecture at the University
of Illinois at Urbana-Champaign. He is the author of numerous books
on the art of light in architecture, including *The Architecture of Natural
Light*, also published by Thames & Hudson.

On the cover: all images © Henry Plummer.
The photographs are reproduced on the following pages: (front) pp. 136–39;
(back, clockwise from top left) pp. 40–43, pp. 30–33, pp. 60–63, pp. 92–95.

On p. 2: Olari Church, Espoo, Finland, 1981, by Käpy and Simo Paavilainen

First published in the United Kingdom in 2012 by
Thames & Hudson Ltd, 181A High Holborn, London WC1V 7QX

First paperback edition 2014

Nordic Light © 2012 Henry Plummer

Art direction and design by Martin Andersen / Andersen M Studio
www.andersenm.com

British Library Cataloguing-in-Publication Data
A catalogue record for this book is available from the British Library
ISBN 978-0-500-29137-5

Printed and bound in China by C & C Offset Printing Co Ltd

To find out about all our publications, please visit **www.thamesandhudson.com**.
There you can subscribe to our e-newsletter, browse or download our current catalogue,
and buy any titles that are in print.

CONTENTS

INTRODUCTION
SEEKING LIGHT IN THE MYSTICAL NORTH

Extreme variations of climate and sun have produced unique conditions of light throughout Scandinavia.[1] The seasons present astonishing swings of illumination. The long, cold winter is dark and gloomy, with the sun barely appearing at all, and when it does, rising and setting for the briefest of times. Night-time permeates into the day to cloak the

Further diffusing the weak sun are atmospheric conditions of unstable weather and frequent clouds that blend into sea air or forest mist. On midsummer evenings, the sun dissolves into an unreal haze that bathes the land in a fairy-like glow, its colours strangely muted and blurred. And during long winter twilights, sky and snow are equally tinged with rainbow hues that linger for hours. While Norway, Sweden, Denmark and Finland are dissimilar in topography and vegetation, their skies share a subdued light that imbues the entire region with mystery. More than the landscape, it is this dream-like atmosphere that tells people at once that they have reached the outermost rim of the earth. Left behind is the brilliant sun of the south, under which shadows are strong and contours sharp, making perception more clear and constant.

Finnish light, Lake Päijänne

Danish clouds and light, Jutland

land in perpetual shade. And during the ecstatic yet fleeting summer, nights are pervaded by the midnight sun, producing almost too much light and concentrating the annual light-fall into several months.

The low slant of sun at high latitudes is also remarkable, transforming human perception with long shadows and strikingly refracted colours – especially in winter, when sunshine arrives at glancing and often peculiar angles. 'One of the qualities of Nordic light', observes Finnish architect Kristian Gullichsen, 'is that in winter it is almost horizontal, and at certain moments comes from below the horizon line. If you are making a drawing with snow on the ground, you put shadows on top, rather than below, the mouldings. Sverre Fehn, the Norwegian master, was especially conscious of the light coming from below and up into a building, and designed for light that was reflected upwards from water or snow.'[2]

These bewitching effects of light were absorbed into Nordic saga and myth, and have permeated the arts. Perhaps their most renowned expression occurred at the end of the nineteenth century, when artists were searching for a way to define their geographic identity at the far edge of Europe. Plein-air painters became obsessed with the muted glow that gives the North its brooding character. This fascination is immediately evident in a series of exhibitions on Scandinavian painting organized in North America and Europe during the 1980s and '90s. Their titles alone are revealing: *Northern Light* (1982–83), *The Mystic North* (1984), *Dreams of a Summer Night* (1986–87) and *The Light of the North* (1995–96).[3] In these collections, drawn from every Nordic land, one is impressed above all by how subtle conditions of natural light, modified by weather, were observed by the artists with painstaking care and depicted on canvas with a kind of devotion.

Apart from the achingly transient summer night, so beautifully captured in Swedish painter Richard Bergh's *Nordic Summer Evening* (1900), artists were enthralled by the soft blur of fog and mist, glistening sheets of translucent ice, pristine blankets of white snow, starry winter nights and the throbbing violets of winter dusk. Portrayed on canvas with penetrating accuracy were the frailest, most evanescent aspects of nature, producing a hypnotic mixture of realism and magic that was completely devoid of sentimentality. Viewers are brought into startling contact with powerful characteristics of light that suffuse the entire picture surface, and are often its primary subject. Drawing ephemera up to the eye are clever manipulations of pictorial space, combining near and far to create a rapport with distant phenomena. This

rugged and richly embellished forms remained somewhat nostalgic in character, and were too physically emphatic to register subtle impacts of light. While spurred along by the modern movement's therapeutic regime of sunlight and fresh air, pioneered in France by Le Corbusier and in Holland by J. J. P. Oud, among others, Scandinavian architects loosened their buildings from the formal and machined stress of Modernism, and sought instead to naturalize simple volumes by suffusing them with a light distinct to the North. Even Alvar Aalto's outwardly rational Viipuri Library (1935), in Vyborg, Russia, for instance, was conceived as a series of 'plateaus', which were illuminated by 'suns in different positions', filling the interior with a 'shadow-free, diffuse light'.[4]

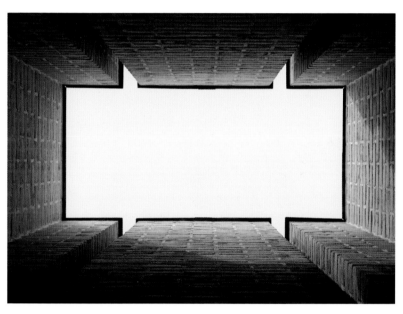

Wall 3, Ballerup, Denmark, 1995, by Per Kirkeby

Århus Town Hall, Denmark, 1942, by Arne Jacobsen

intimacy also appears in genre painting, adding a mystical intensity to urban scenes, as well as quiet domestic interiors. Even in pictures of ordinary life, we find ethereal light washing into barren rooms to bring every surface under its spell, as it melts away contours and hangs in the air. Often referred to as 'mood paintings', these pictures convey a contemplative space in which separate details have lost significance, and light has harmonized all the parts into a resonant whole.

By the 1920s and '30s, Scandinavia's early masters of modern architecture – Erik Bryggman and Alvar Aalto in Finland, Gunnar Asplund and Sigurd Lewerentz in Sweden, and Arne Jacobsen in Denmark – were beginning to explore a vision of reality that was similar to that of the plein-air painters of the previous century. Their efforts to construct a Nordic identity that was authentic to its place in the world drew a sharp contrast with the earlier National Romantic movement, whose

In their efforts to seize upon Nordic light as a source of identity and inspiration, architects were faced with a dilemma that is unique to frigid climates. At high latitudes, where daylight is meagre and solidity is needed to resist the harsh winters, how could interiors be generously lit and brought into contact with the pageantry of nature? In response to this problem, a variety of architectural forms were developed that closely linked rooms with the sky – forms that were able to collect, preserve and allocate the scant illumination, while putting its changing moods on display as a metaphysical image of the North. Building profiles were moulded to gather low angles of light, and as much as possible from the south – the only part of the sky where the sun is present in winter. For buildings demanding softer light, such as museums and libraries, sunlight was tempered by multiple reflections, or diffuse illumination was garnered from northerly parts of the sky. To achieve this control over incident light, building plans and sections were shaped virtually into funnels, aimed to specific points on the horizon, and hollowed within to conduct captured light to rooms where it was most needed. By transforming architecture into an optical instrument, a proficient use could be made of scarce daylight and every room exposed to the sky. A further virtue of these building forms is their revelation of the solar forces unique to high latitudes, telling people *where* they are and anchoring them into a particular place on the planet.

Complementing the inhalation of precious light is another characteristic of Scandinavian architecture – the monolithic use of pale materials to conserve and magnify faint illumination. Reflective finishes, from white plaster and blond wood to ceramic tile and silvery concrete,

frail Nordic light washes over these bare rooms, a connection is felt with the sun, moon or clouds, without having to see them directly.

The Scandinavian urge to live in close communion with nature can be partly explained by the survival of a rural society until well into the twentieth century. A strong relationship with the elements developed from aeons of living alone in the wilderness – closely bound to the seasons and weather, immersed in eternal darkness and ice, which are overcome each spring by the returning sun. The artist Richard Bergh aptly described this imprint on the northern spirit: 'The landscape, that tract in which we live, affects our lives, not just in the superficial sense of enforcing on us certain fixed living conditions, but also by the purely suggestive influence it has on our soul. That drama that daily is

Tapiola Church, Finland, 1965, by Aarno Ruusuvuori

Dust Motes Dancing in Sunlight, 1900, by Vilhelm Hammershøi

avoid the premature absorption of light, while helping to spread illumination to every corner of the space. Beyond its practical value, the pale finish serves a more poetic aim – as a projection screen upon which subtle daylight can be exhibited, and even intensified. Delicate illumination becomes more visible on neutral and reflective walls, in the same way that diluted pigments are fully revealed on white canvas. As the

in front of our eyes puts its mark on our inner being. ... Every landscape is a state of mind.'[5]

Nordic architects have long been resourceful in nurturing this 'state of mind' by etching it into the everyday buildings in which people live. In addition to 'painting' rooms with the moods of the sky, another means of transmuting nature into architecture is metaphoric evocation.

As daylight passes through windows and bathes over walls, it can be modulated to echo the characteristics of light that identify the North, and in doing so directs its appeal to the poetic imagination, rather than the rational mind. Metaphors suggestive of natural phenomena resonate with images that arouse the human psyche, causing the beholder to conjure up ephemera beyond the reach of the physical eye. Even monumental vernacular buildings are made aware of their universe: the dark intensity of the Norwegian stave church, which arouses an image of black winter skies dotted with stars; the billowing white vaults of a Danish church, which stirs an impression of the dramatic cloud forms unique to that land; or the peasant log hut, whose tonal vibrations suggest the primeval forests that still cover much of Scandinavia.

fied abstraction of light and place that has evolved over the past century, based on lyrical images that are devoid of use and unconcerned with formal beauty, serving instead to reawaken the imagination and stimulate a more active role in its harmonious relationships with nature. This process underlies Alvar Aalto's fascination with thickets of poles and sinuous screens, which allude to the cleft light of the Finnish forest, or walls coated with rippling tiles that recall the play of light across a lake's surface, in either case without resort to literal imitations of nature. The resulting kinship with the environment is based more on interpretation than resemblance, and operates at a deeper level than the easy, somewhat superficial solidarity with nature in folk architecture. By embracing contemporary values of ambiguity and self-realization, these

Dipoli Student Assembly Building, Otaniemi, Finland, 1966, by Reima Pietilä

The architectural production of these primitive echoes is obviously driven by something deeper and more vital than pragmatic necessity or aesthetic desire. Beneath the impulse to commune with the sky is a longing for elemental modes of life, confirming that one exists somewhere, and that one exists *emotionally* and *spiritually*, as well as physically. This search for reality is increasingly evident in the intensi-

elusive metaphors invite us to intuit and decipher their latent images, and in the process exercise our own capacity to creatively 'see'. Communicable images of this kind – which arouse the dreaming consciousness, helping people to recapture a direct experience of reality and to understand where they belong – are a pervasive theme in the past century of Nordic architecture. Examples are legion, among them the

In recent decades, this poetic tradition has grown ever more obscure yet involving, using pure geometry and severe austerity to defamiliarize architecture from nature, and reinforcing this divergence with industrial materials or coats of paint. The sublimation of image and memory in the management of northern light continues to tease out something of significance, rather than forming it in an obvious manner. By expanding the field of human perception, these faint evocations become far more demanding and intriguing, and ultimately powerful, than formal analogy – challenging the human faculty to create images that exceed each person's immediate memory. We find these extra depths of imaginative power in the overlapping white planes of Juha Leiviskä's buildings, for instance, as well as in the recursive and rectilinear wood-

Seinäjoki Church, Finland, 1960, by Alvar Aalto

Main building, Helsinki Institute of Technology, Otaniemi, Finland, 1964, by Alvar Aalto

metaphoric skies constructed by Gunnar Asplund over his Woodland Chapel (1920), in Stockholm's Skogskyrkogården, and Stockholm City Library (1927; pp. 77, 81), or the undulating vaults that pile up and drift over ceilings in Arne Jacobsen's Århus Town Hall (1942; pp. 7, 52) and Jørn Utzon's Bagsværd Church (1976; p. 56), both in Denmark. Then there is the recollection of arctic night in the dark brickwork and shadowy voids of the Swedish churches of Sigurd Lewerentz and Peter Celsing, or in the faceted light on battered concrete used by Reima Pietilä to commemorate Finland's glacial origins.

work of Sverre Fehn, or the steel meshes and dark metal boxes of Helsinki firm Heikkinen-Komonen. The non-representational images formed by these architects transcend the level of metaphor, to charm and activate deeper strata of the human psyche. By freeing its evocations from any quick and docile memory, architecture expands the creative scope of the eye, as well as the imagination, asking people to sense, rather than see, that they are still in contact with ultimate reality.

The existential achievements of Scandinavian architecture, which explain the world to which they belong, should not allow us to overlook their contribution to an international discourse on light that over the past century has reshaped our understanding of architecture.[6] While we cannot imagine the finest Nordic buildings appearing anywhere else in the world, neither can we imagine them before the revolution of thought and feeling that gave rise to modernity. Iconic works such as Aalto's Villa Mairea (1941; pp. 104, 132), along with Jacobsen's National Bank of Denmark (1971; p. 184) and Fehn's Hedmark Museum (1979 and 2006; p. 86) are distinctly northern interpretations of the modern belief that light can have a presence of its own – where it is free, in part, of its illuminating role, and even its past symbolic value.

Laying the foundation for this contemporary understanding of light was a transformational shift a century ago in our comprehension of

Main building, Helsinki Institute of Technology, Otaniemi, Finland, 1964, by Alvar Aalto

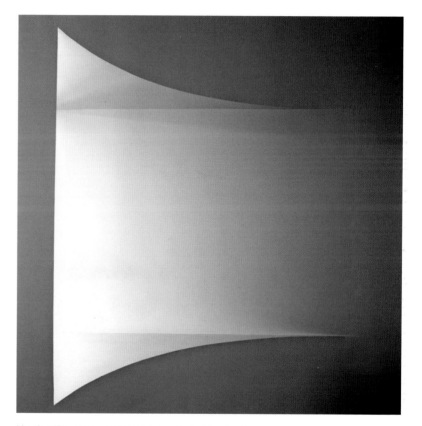

Herning IBA, Herning, Denmark, 1995, by Henning Larsen

light itself. A series of discoveries, including Albert Einstein's conception of light as particles of energy called 'photons', put forward in 1905, together with physicist Max Planck's theory of quantum physics and James Clerk Maxwell's observation that light behaves as an electromagnetic wave, altered our Newtonian view of light. Emerging in the process was a new kind of light that exists as both wave and photon – a 'modern light', as it was called, of the twentieth century. Anticipating the revelations that air and matter are vibrant with energy were artists envisioning similar phenomena. In the smoke and mist of Claude

Monet's paintings, the dissolving away of figural form allowed light itself, and its interweaving colours and shadows, to become the predominant subject. Many artists focused on particulate light, and the complex interaction of light with matter. Pointillist painters Georges Seurat and Paul Signac covered their canvases with dots of complementary colours, immersing half-dissolved figures in an atomized glow that caused the picture field to quiver and appear more luminous than it actually was. And in the paintings of Vincent van Gogh, light exists as trembling particles of radiant pigment, which emanate in concentric waves from a sulphur-yellow sun or star, lamp or candle. Orphic painter Robert Delaunay summed up these efforts: 'So long as art is subservient to objects, it remains description, literature.' The way beyond this is for light itself to be 'treated as an independent means of representation'.[7]

Continuing to construe a reality in which light is more autonomous and tangible than previously thought, abstract painting becomes virtually objectless and devoid of representation, so that the only figure left is light itself and its infinite modulations. In the radically anti-materialist images of American painters Richard Pousette-Dart, Mark Tobey, Mark Rothko and Barnett Newman, ambient light is carried to a state of almost mystical purity. The physical world has fallen silent and vanished, leaving behind an elusive, spiritual atmosphere. In their

most famously his *Dust Motes Dancing in Sunlight* (1900; p. 8), where walls are seen through palpable rays of slanting sun, and there exists in space a violet-tinged glow that is far more arresting and alive than its solid backdrop. A similar dream-like space that tests the limits of physical reality was explored by Finnish painter Ellen Thesleff (opposite), whose pictures are filled with a silver-grey mist that serves as a vehicle of introspection. Equally pensive is Danish artist Peder Severin Krøyer's blue haze, which hangs over Skagen on summer evenings, or the transcendental blues of winter nights amid icy mountains of Norwegian painter Harald Sohlberg. The throbbing blue air of winter night that suffuses Stockholm's buildings and streets was the subject for Swedish artist Eugène Jansson, showing the city's liquefaction into a place of

Vor Frue Church, Copenhagen, Denmark, 1829, by C. F. Hansen

President's Residence, Mäntyniemi, Finland, 1993, by Reima Pietilä

installations, beginning in the 1960s, artists Robert Irwin and James Turrell made even a room seem substanceless, unless one means the vaporous substance of light itself.

While Scandinavian artists have taken part in this search for truth, there was less need to invent a new mode of painting, since the Nordic world is inherently veiled by molecular light drifting through space. The reality portrayed by Nordic painters is physically present, but reduced to the setting for a luminescence that hangs in the air and penetrates objects. Consider the starkly empty rooms of Vilhelm Hammershøi,

hallucinatory beauty. Northern sculptors, constrained by matter, have been no less inclined to turn solid form into a scaffold for palpable light, as in the brick constructions of Per Kirkeby (see p. 7), or the timber blocks of Kain Tapper, carved to imitate moonlight or morning mist, and the aluminium slats of Raimo Utriainen, which dissolved into a shimmer of lines.

In their comparable efforts to elevate light to an independent medium closely attuned to geographic reality, Nordic architects are producing buildings that are true not only to their place in the world,

Aspens, 1893, by Ellen Thesleff

but also to our current age. The twentieth-century proposition that the forces, energies and intensities of light are a new measure of the world we live in, and that architecture offers a venue for these agitations, reaches what is arguably its fullest and most convincing expression in Scandinavia – in buildings based on a formal restraint to enhance the flux and fragile beauty of natural light. The bare and elemental simplicity so universally admired in this architecture serves an aim beyond itself, allowing its designers to loosen light from the physical objects with which it mingles, and in the process to liberate light itself from its duty as an instrument of definition, and assume a more commanding role in buildings.

If the art of building in the far north has lagged behind the spatial and formal ingenuity of Western Europe and America, it has nevertheless been at the forefront of the metaphysical aspirations of twentieth- and twenty-first-century architecture. A telling sign of this leadership is its close parallel with, and at times anticipation of, the work of artists who use light as a means of expression, rather than merely for illuminating objects (Thomas Wilfred's *Lumia* recitals of the 1920s, László Moholy-Nagy's *Light Prop*, finished in 1930, and Otto Piene's *Light Ballets* of the 1960s), while adapting these themes to everyday life and harnessing their flow to the passing sky. Scandinavia's utterly simple and austere buildings, where airborne light exists in its own right and lives its own drama, have also prefigured the meditative calm and glowing nothingness produced by installation artists of recent decades: Robert Irwin's dissolution of material into light; James Turrell's efforts to make light material, and to create an experience rather than an object; and the mesmerizing environments of Olafur Eliasson, including *Weather Project* (2003), which filled the Turbine Hall at London's Tate Modern with a fine mist, pervaded by yellow light.

Clearly expressed in Scandinavia's most sublime buildings of the past century is a serious contemplation of Nordic light in the context of the contemporary world. At the heart of this still-emerging vision are the animating powers of immaterial forces and energy, which are able to resonate within each living observer, bringing us closer to the human essence of architecture. Instead of fixed images that are passively viewed, light is used to produce fluid images that arouse a creative human response, and can change the heart and mind of an active, feeling and moving beholder. This non-objective aim is well stated by Finnish architect Juhani Pallasmaa, who notes that 'nowadays I don't regard architecture as a building in itself; it is a means of revealing something else. For me, light is the most ecstatic architectural experience there is, and in many ways the best architecture is a preparation for the experience of light.'[8]

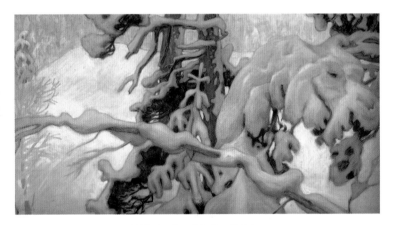

Landscape Under Snow, 1902, by Akseli Gallen-Kallela

1

WHITENESS

The pristine beauty and illuminating power of
pure, white volumes

The white luminosity that is often present in Scandinavian architecture is, in part, a direct response to the arctic climate. There are obvious practical advantages to a white finish, for pale rooms remain faintly lit even over the long, dark winter, offering sanctuary from the gloom until the skies brighten in spring. But the extraordinary whiteness that has taken hold in Nordic architecture, above all in Denmark and Finland, cannot be fully explained by pragmatic need alone. This peaceful radiance, devoid of matter, touches a chord in the human soul. By maximizing light and dissolving objects into energy, white things glow with an intensity beyond that of coloured objects. White rooms offer a means to stay near the most elusive aspects of nature: delicate skylight and mercurial weather, and the shifting moods of the hours and seasons.

around a tree, and thus conveys an important truth – that northern snows accumulate and drift into massive volumes with an imminent vitality, personified further by the moods of the sky.

Among the forerunners in Scandinavia's genealogy of white architecture are Denmark's medieval churches, whose soft, subtle radiance is especially intimate in parish churches such as that in the village of Elmelunde (opposite), on the island of Møn, in which the whitewash of low vaulting makes the transparent frescoes more luminous and brings their unearthly beauty close to the congregation below. White light is purified further in the medieval cathedrals at Odense and Århus, and above all at Maribo (opposite), on the island of Lolland, where walls and vaults are united in a state of oneness, setting them off as a heavenly

Church of the Assumption, Riola di Vergato, Italy, 1978, by Alvar Aalto

Opstandelses Church, Albertslund, Denmark, 1984, by Inger and Johannes Exner

The affection for whiteness is also linked to the pristine beauty of snow-covered landscapes. The first winter snowfall transforms the dark earth, lifting the mood of city and countryside alike. In what other part of the world could there be a word for first snow (*ensilumi* in Finnish) or a poet write: 'Each snowflake's fall is a sign of homecoming'?[9] The same joy is immediately evident in paintings of winter scenes, in which a fresh mantle of snow and its soft gleam are the very essence of the picture. In *Landscape Under Snow* (1902; p. 14), Akseli Gallen-Kallela portrayed a sensuous whiteness that appears almost alive as it wraps and curls

realm above the praying masses. Gentle light from aisle windows is endlessly modelled as it plays over the manifold volumes, casting faint shadows in the webbing of vaults, thrown into relief by highlit ribs, while the faceted piers and soffits of arches are brightened or dimmed according to their orientation. Even the rigid geometry of nineteenth-century Danish classicism, epitomized by C. F. Hansen's Vor Frue Church (1829; p. 12), in Copenhagen, is soothed by transparent shadows and gradations of white light, whose brilliance increases with height to draw the eye upwards.

Urging along the twentieth-century evolution of Scandinavia's culture of whiteness was the architecture of early Modernism, and its equation of whiteness with health and wellbeing. Yet when Alvar Aalto began to envelop his buildings in a pure-white finish in the 1920s and '30s, he took great pains to avoid Modernism's absolute forms and harsh gleam, instead massaging his white containers to endow them with subtleties harmonious with the human psyche. This reasoned approach to maximizing sun and air, seen at his Paimio Sanatorium (1933; p. 21), in Finland, was complemented by an equal concern for humanizing the hospital environment with a cushioned whiteness that conveyed empathy. Smoothly rounded white volumes were outlined with luminous colours to guide movement: accents of blue and grey around doors,

which light shades gradually into half-tones to yield vague outlines and hazy forms. These relaxed effects appear both in large volumes, including the rounded edges of the Paimio Sanatorium's façades, and in such small details as the fireplace recess at the Villa Mairea (1941; pp. 104, 132), in Noormarkku, Finland. Aalto would eventually apply this soft–hard quality of plaster to entire rooms, creating white voids that arouse an image of shelter reminiscent of animal burrows in winter snow, or a peasant house buried in snowdrifts – images that hold a primal allure for the Nordic mind. The continuous plasticity of sinuous voids in his church at Riola di Vergato (1978; opposite) shifts attention away from the container, and onto pale tones collecting in and washing over the pristine finish. Instead of a uniform glow, we find a varied light that

Maribo Cathedral, Lolland, Denmark, 15th century

Elmelunde Church, Møn, Denmark, 15th century

elevators and handrails, and daffodil-yellow linoleum underfoot, flowing through the reception area and up the staircase beyond to provide a hint of sunshine and offset the despair of disease. This cheerful message reappears in Jokela & Kareoja's Government Office Building (1992; p. 224), also in Finland, where the ambient whiteness serves as a foil for small accents of primary colour.[10]

The white stucco of Aalto's later buildings was gradually softened by a repertoire of sinuous contours and cavities. In contrast to the machined whiteness of Modernism, Aalto developed a curvaceous sfumato in

sprays over the cavity in a painterly way, fogging the shell by extending beyond the edges of things and dying away in empty space.

While never attaining the pliancy or comprehensiveness of Aalto, Gunnar Asplund and Arne Jacobsen used small concentrations of gentle, white curves to caress light and slowly shade tonalities into one another. Asplund's use of sfumato was generally limited to incidental textures or details, such as the tiny shadows on rippling plaster that muffle the white drum of the Stockholm City Library (1927; pp. 77, 81), or the supple white columns of the Göteborg Law Courts (1937), which were produced by moulding a magnesium mixture into sinuous shapes around the steel. Plasticity was of greater concern to Jacobsen at Århus Town Hall (1942; pp. 7, 52), where the diffuse illumination from skylights is soothed further by gently contoured ceilings and columns that are devoid of all the sharp shadows of early Modernism. In recent decades, this Danish affinity for mild white tones has been explored through other geometries, such as in the helical ramps of the ARoS Art Museum (2004), also in Århus, by Schmidt Hammer Lassen, or the gently sagging vaults of the Utzon Centre (2008), by Jørn and Kim Utzon.

Paralleling these curvaceous traditions is a rival approach, where sharp-edged but repetitive planes or cells are used to create incremental monochrome shadings, reminding us once again that in the North

Jyväskylä, to Reima Pietilä's white voids for the residence for the president of Finland (1993; pp. 12, 49), at Mäntyniemi. The high point in this constructive dispersal of radiant fragments is the collaged white architecture of Juha Leiviskä. Buildings such as the Myyrmäki Church (1984; p. 22), Vallila Library (1991; p. 20) and the Church of the Good Shepherd (2002; p. 68), all near Helsinki, are based upon a superimposition of points, lines and planes that are slightly displaced and overlaid to catch varied amounts of light on a uniformly immaculate finish. The essential point in all of these structures is the way a pervasive white glow enables broken volumes to transcend their otherwise fragmentary perception, and attain a unity of being while restoring the essential unity between man and nature.

German Embassy, Helsinki, Finland, 1993, by Juha Leiviskä

Bank of Sweden, Stockholm, Sweden, 1976, by Peter Celsing

there is no such thing as absolute white. Light loses its naturalistic function of modelling form, and is instead fractured into shades that are strewn across and interlock with splintered volumes. Aalto at times showed an inclination in this regard, from the multi-angled wings of the Paimio Sanatorium to the folded grids of white marble at his Enso-Gutzeit Office Building (1962), in Helsinki. More boldly defined are the staggered façades of Jacobsen's Bellavista Housing Complex (1934) in Copenhagen, which were shaped to increase sea views while producing a crystalline multiplicity similar to that of Cubist paintings. More recent efforts to bring a gem-like brilliance to white light are being led by Finnish architects seeking a path away from Aalto's sinuosity, from the honey-combed cells of Eero Valjakka's Lounaisrinne Housing (1985), in

Though never abandoning a figural and somewhat classical weight, the white voids of Danish architect Henning Larsen are pleasantly disturbed and rendered ambiguous by tensions between porous layers. The flat, white walls of his Copenhagen Business School (1989; p. 26) are perceptually charged by windows pierced through successive linings, allowing different amounts and qualities of light to be juxtaposed and appear simultaneously. This shuttling between two domains is occasionally excited by a strong colour, so that the white frame and isolated hue make the stratification enticing, even hypnotic. An entirely different mode of collage appears in Larsen's Ny Carlsberg Glyptotek Addition (1996; p. 92), also in Copenhagen, where white light gains material density through an interplay of closely matched materials and finishes.

Light and shade grow soft around the staircase of rounded white marble, while the silky white plaster walls possess the translucence of Venetian *stucco lustro*. To avoid glare upon the latter, its planes were impressed with shallow recesses, whose slight reveals give further depth to the mistily glowing surface. The seeds of this alchemic idea were sown by Aalto as far back as the 1930s, in his interweaving of white-painted plaster, white-enamelled steel and smooth white linoleum at the Paimio Sanatorium to give material substance to immaterial light, a quality that peaks in his Nordjyllands Art Museum (1972; p. 30), in Denmark, where every finish offers a different shade of white.

At another Danish building, Jørn Utzon's Bagsværd Church (1976; p. 56), expanding the intonations of whiteness and solving needs of light

Anshelm's polarity of light, which, to use the words of Gaston Bachelard in *The Poetics of Space*, 'rises upward' and 'differentiates itself in terms of its verticality',[12] is more subtly developed at Malmö Konsthall (1976; p. 214), where the cellular sparkle overhead is underpinned by flat, white walls and a rough timber floor of coarse, bleached planks, rooting the skyward tones in a pale but earthly ground.

The idea that modelled light on a tactile white surface can test the boundaries between the physical and the metaphysical unites Danish buildings as different as Inger and Johannes Exner's Opstandelses Church (1984; pp. 16, 150), with its sidelit brick relief, and the textile-like concrete walls of Steven Holl's Herning Museum of Contemporary Art (2009; p. 34). These limits were questioned more gently by Järvinen

Tapiola Cultural Centre, Finland, 1989, by Arto Sipinen

preservation were dual concerns from the outset.[11] Finishes range from the 'heavenly light' of the pure white cylindrical shells of thin concrete, finely etched with shade by the formwork, to the muted off-whites of a sanctified ground: the latexed sheen of precast concrete floor planks and pulpit slabs; the bleached timber of grilles and pews; and the white-painted brick of an altar screen. A drier, more astringent whiteness, set on a base of grey and black, also brings an awareness of gravity to Klas Anshelm's Swedish museums. The monochromaticism of his Lund Konsthall (1957; p. 205) is stretched out by angling ceilings and walls with respect to skylights, giving each a slightly different ratio of diffuse and reflected light. These Cubist arrays gradually shade into mirror-like floors of dark grey stone and the black-painted lustre of stair railings.

& Airas at their Suna School (1985; p. 207), in Espoo, Finland, where multiple textures push and pull on a uniform skin of white paint. A low relief of different materials – with textures that range from smooth to grainy, contrasting flatness with assemblies of battens, frames or grids – imprint slightly different shades of white in the uniform sheen from underneath. 'The light is like glue,' architect Kari Järvinen observed. 'It pulls everything in the space together. The ribs and strips make the light into a material, so that you can see it. You can feel that the real light is coming in.'[13] The few colours present, pale beige and lustrous blue, seem only shadows within the placid, white light. Like a snow-dusted landscape, the latexed finish turns a little fuzzy to the eye, as the unified tones perceptually advance and recede.

Beyond its inherent Nordic appeal, a membranous coat of white paint over contrasting textures draws on a broader set of notions in twentieth-century art. By sharing in the mystery of objects submerged beneath a luminous cloak, it arouses some of the dreamy state we find in the 'crates' of American sculptor Louise Nevelson, whose 'found objects' were originally painted a uniform black, and in later work white or gold, to simultaneously shroud and unite the disparate fragments and endow them with enigmatic power. A similar impact occurs in abstract paintings where cryptic things surge up beneath a luminous white skin: Kazimir Malevich's *White on White* (1918); Barnett Newman's attempts to 'dig into metaphysical secrets' with white washes on canvas; or Robert Ryman's swirling impastos of white paint that change with the light.

Vallila Library, Helsinki, Finland, 1991, by Juha Leiviskä

More volumetric are Christo's wrapped objects, for which the artist uses a continuous shroud of reflective fabric to transmute and elevate dry reality, thus coming close to the Nordic impulse to invent as well as conceal with light, leaving mysteries beneath a half-awake glow.

The desire to ground ethereal whiteness by rooting it back into the earth has long been a theme of Finnish architecture. The dazzling white cubes of the Tapiola Cultural Centre (1989; p. 19) by Arto Sipinen, for instance, are anchored into the forest town and glacial landscape by a terraced plinth of intermediate tones – a geologic substratum of white quartz, pale sandstone and pitted, white travertine slabs. Stone is again

the transitional vehicle at Leiviskä's German Embassy (1993; p. 18), in Helsinki. The impeccable white finish of the rooms mingles into the outdoor terrace and landscape beyond through an interleaved sequence of columns and walls, ending with planes of grey German limestone set on a podium of grey Finnish granite. The bleak and chilly atmosphere of this whitish grey knitting, where pure-white tones phase into a mineral base, has a desolate beauty similar to that of the Nordic winter.

The antithetical idea of secreting white voids away in an earthen crust draws poetry from a different source – wrappings such as tree bark and woollen coats, where something inwardly delicate is buffered from the world by a rough outer lining. Exploiting this primal allure are buildings whose white cavities are secluded within and glimpsed through a dark envelope, allowing their luminous cores to be anticipated, discovered, metaphorically opened, and then later resonate in the memory. Offering this kind of atavistic pleasure are the brick churches of Käpy and Simo Paavilainen at Espoo (1981; pp. 2, 218) and Juha Leiviskä at Kuopio (1992; p. 154) and Pakila (2002; p. 68), in Finland, as well as those of Regnbuen Arkitekter at Antvorskov (2005; p. 36) and Dybkær (2010; p. 40), in Denmark, all of whose glowing, white hollows appear through cracks in a reddish crust. In the context of religious architecture, of course, this opposition manifests an ontological thirst beyond that of shelter. Making an analogy with the human body and its innermost soul, these churches visualize two modes of being – the profane and the sacred, the former belonging to the earth and the latter to heaven.

Making a Swedish contribution to the theme of introverted whiteness, whose beauty is internal rather than external, is Peter Celsing's Bank of Sweden (1976; p. 18), in Stockholm. Rugged plates of black granite present a grim and foreboding countenance, but closer scrutiny uncovers a glimmer beneath the dark mask – glassy windows with smooth, granite mullions have been slightly displaced from the outer holes, initiating a shift from dark to light, closed to open, rough to smooth, while subverting the outwardly dour mass with a playful motif of paper-thin layers. Culminating this lightening mood and hidden softness is the communal space atop the building, its joyful attic lined with materials that are friendly to skin. Some rooms are finished with pale birchwood or Venetian *stucco lustro*, but the dominant substance is hand-formed white tile. Conjured up in these rooms is one of mankind's most touching images: a quiet seashell, where a tough outer mantle safeguards the inward appeal of a smooth, white chamber.[14] We seem to only half-remember this creature comfort, which bypasses rational thought and appeals directly to muscle and skin, playing on an animal urge to withdraw to a place that is far removed from hostile forces – all the better to express a building besieged by arctic winters.

Paimio Sanatorium, Finland, 1933, by Alvar Aalto

MYYRMÄKI CHURCH
VANTAA, FINLAND, 1984
BY JUHA LEIVISKÄ

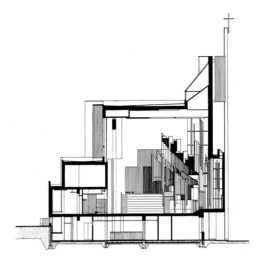

The interleaving of pure white planes at multiple scales in this Finnish church shifts all awareness to the cold, white light that seeps between them and clings to their surface. Great effort has gone into harmonizing an infinite range of pristine tones, owing to the varying amounts of illumination that are shed on the planes at any given moment. Further differentiating the glow are contrasting textures beneath a uniform coat of white paint: smooth plaster, hard metal, grainy woodwork and thin slats, all of which are complemented by diaphanous white fabrics, set around the altar. Virtually all material colour has been eliminated to produce an exquisite emptiness with a luminosity that shimmers softly, beckoning. The few spots of colour above the brick floor – blue seat cushions and golden lamps – are celestial in tone. Otherwise every bare surface is absolutely white, from walls and ceilings to pews and furnishings, even altar and pulpit, along with the narrow mullions of windows and skylights. Immediately soothing to human nerves, even vaguely sedative, the space envelops churchgoers in an achingly beautiful whiteness.

Above Overall view from the east; *top* Transverse section, looking south; *left* Plan

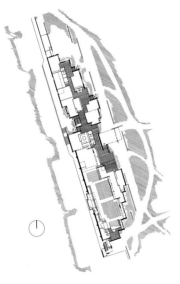

Upward view of windows in the east wall

Detail of the choir

View looking north past the pulpit and altar

Altar from the east

View from the west, across the nave to the entrance

Overall view looking north from the choir

Enfilades of openings in punctured white walls

COPENHAGEN BUSINESS SCHOOL
FREDERIKSBERG, DENMARK, 1989
BY HENNING LARSEN

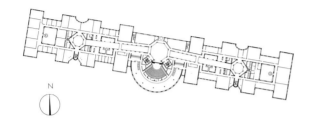

The concentrated glow within the school's interior 'street' derives from the zenithal light that pours into a white vessel of punctured walls and latticed rails, set on a floor of polished black and white stone. The shifting geometry of round columns and curved ceilings against predominantly flat walls adds soft gradations to the sharp tonal contrasts of planes and openings. But it is the layering of apertures in successive walls that largely determines the character of whiteness. Windows and holes in the multilayered planes align with each other, while receding into corridors or rooms with additional perforations beyond, encouraging the eye to probe through a series of white tissues that brighten or dim against foreground planes. White-on-white patterns and their surface tensions are viewed through one another, and overlap in the manner of a collage. As light showers the immaculate street and trickles through its punctured planes, it brings about a shifting play and frequent reversal of figure and ground, stimulating the imagination as the eye discovers scraps of reality taken out of context. Complicating these luminous cells are transitional zones painted blue or pink, hues that frame or isolate white light, and bring a mesmerizing force to the enfilades through which human eyes are constantly peering.

Above Pink octagonal node at the west end of the interior street; *top* Upper-level plan

View of the interior street, from the west

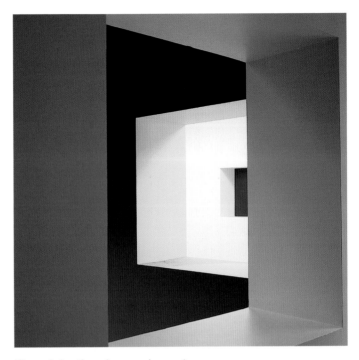

Diagonal view through successive apertures

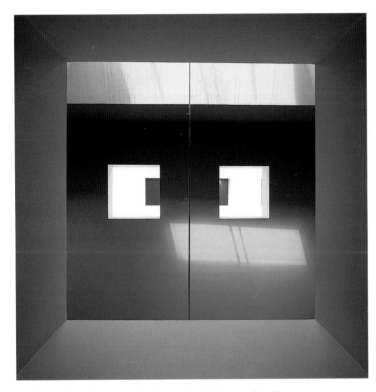

Axial view through consecutive blue and white layers of wall

Skylights and perforated walls at the upper level of one of the niches

Light-guiding scoops over the central hall

NORDJYLLANDS ART MUSEUM
AALBORG, DENMARK, 1972
BY ALVAR AALTO AND JEAN-JACQUES BARUËL

The museum's austere yet paradoxically rich atmosphere is created by the varied lighting of a broad palette of white materials and textures. White paint covers most of the walls and ceilings, as well as the scoops and blades of skylights that direct illumination, imparting a full gamut of shadows to the diverse curvatures and planes. Beneath this plasticity is a finer scale of light modulation on the differing textures of plaster and concrete, brick and wood. Adding lustrous notes to the drier ambience are polished floors of white Carrara marble, along with the enamelled gleam of metalwork and lamp fixtures. The building clearly transcends the museum cliché of a neutral white container for exhibiting art, for its drawn-out tones are inherently involving without being distracting. Beyond displaying the hours and seasons, as well as passing weather, the whiteness further links visitors to place through metaphoric evocation, suggesting the delicate play of light on clouds and snow, whose dream-provoking images help to anchor people in a greater world of space.

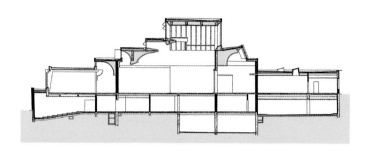

Above Open-plan east galleries; *top* Section through the south gallery, central exhibition hall and north gallery; *below* Longitudinal section, through the open-plan east galleries

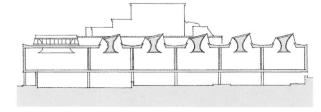

Upward view in the central hall for temporary exhibitions

View to the clerestories and ceiling of the central hall

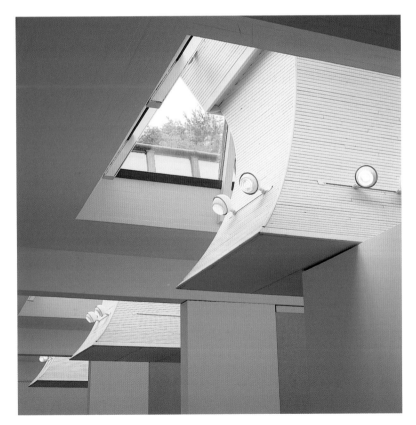

Successive light-scoops over the east galleries

View through successive east galleries

Partitioned east gallery

Textile imprints in white concrete

HERNING MUSEUM OF CONTEMPORARY ART
HERNING, DENMARK, 2009
BY STEVEN HOLL

Expanding the language of whiteness at this museum building are irregular imprints on the concrete walls, produced by using a formwork lined with uneven truck tarps to stamp a relief that appears rumpled and, at close range, canvas-like. The crinkled shadows, which deepen and colour as sunlight moves over each skewed plane, were inspired in part by the *Achrome* series of the late 1950s and early '60s by Italian artist Piero Manzoni, many of which were made at the museum and remain in its permanent collection. Manzoni's wonderfully haptic textures were generated with rough gesso, impregnations of kaolin and glue, and at times cotton padding and fluffy fibreglass, so as to criss-cross the glowing white surface with shadowy wrinkles and bulges, stitchings and grooves. While the museum interior has a welcoming softness, owing to curved vaults that deliver light, it is the exterior bonding of light to matter that stays in the memory, as well as the skin.

Overall view from the southeast

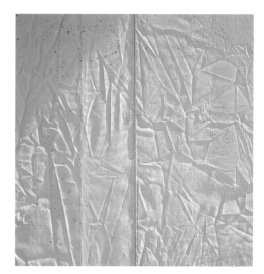

Imprinted concrete, tinged by the late-afternoon sun

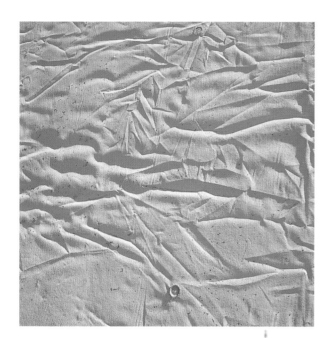

Imprinted concrete texture

Upward view of the northwest façade

South aisle

Convergent streams of immaculate light

ANTVORSKOV CHURCH
SLAGELSE, DENMARK, 2005
BY REGNBUEN ARKITEKTER

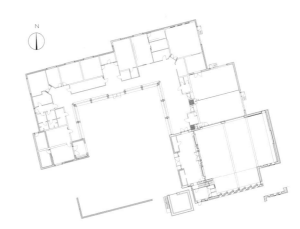

Hidden within a crust of red brick is a space brimming with pure, white light that brightens gradually towards the altar, where it streams in from a slit in the roof and small side windows. As at Jørn Utzon's Bagsværd Church (1976; p. 56), also in Denmark, the cloud-like ceiling rises as it drifts towards the altar, to echo the spiritual journey below, a flow that is repeated in the baffled walls along the south aisle. The ceiling slats and brick texture are highly responsive to glancing light, injecting a delicate shadow play in the larger tones they construct. Nuancing light around the altar are distinctive openings in all three walls. Admitting a low pool of northern light is a window set at floor level, while four small embrasures with stained glass to the south tinge their illumination with differing hues. Immediately behind the altar is a vertical channel that is bevelled to catch slightly more light than its neighbouring planes, marking the holiest point in the church as the centre of a blank triptych, while making a vertical link with the heavens.

Above Altar recess; *top* Plan; *below* Longitudinal section, looking south

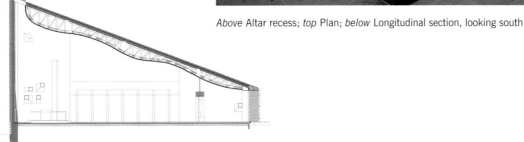

Low window in the northeast corner

Detail of windows with coloured glass

Inscribed and folded shapes of whiteness

DYBKÆR CHURCH
SILKEBORG, DENMARK, 2010
BY REGNBUEN ARKITEKTER

Enveloping Dybkær Church, also by Regnbuen Arkitekter (see Antvorskov Church; p. 36), are gradations of white light that are not sensed as one, but many in one. The calm and restful atmosphere varies from the central nave, whose growing brightness draws attention towards the altar, to side aisles with differing character – the north indirectly lit and enveloped in a white fog, while the south is sidelit and linked to the sun with sharp alternations of light and shadow. The immaculate glow around the altar is modulated to further enchant, while focusing the observing eye. Illumination arrives from three directions: low from the north to emphasize a black steel crucifix; more broadly from the south as a glancing wash; and as a shower directly behind the altar, guided down through a sluice of wall. Reminiscent of the 'white writing' of American artist Mark Tobey, the nave walls are animated by tiny and barely noticed vibrations – the irregular texture of brickwork along with tiny hatchings of script-like lines from the holes for acoustic treatment. These filigrees turn the surface into a medium compounded of light and shade, its network of fine lines expressive of contemplative experience.

Nave from the west

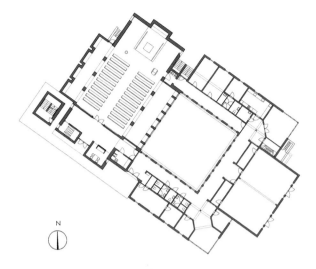

N

Altar recess

Above View across the nave to the north aisle; *top* Ground-level plan

Northeast window and crucifix

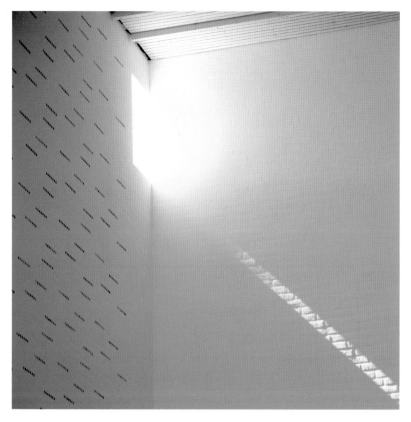

Southwest window with late-morning sun

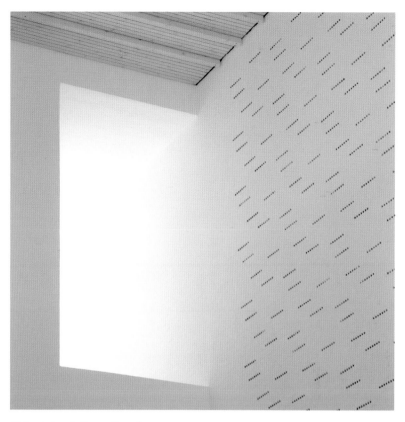

High window in the northwest corner

South aisle from the east

Baffled corner window

Seinäjoki Church, Finland, 1960, by Alvar Aalto

2

RHYTHM

The embodiment of the pulse of nature in vibrating
patterns of light

Scandinavians have intuitively grasped that the innermost essence of natural forms lies not in their outward shape, but in something deeper and more mysterious: the energy that brings the world alive. The earthen terrain stretches and twists over time, rock stratifies and erodes, water flows and cascades, clouds move and reshape with the wind, and mist concentrates in dense fog, only to disperse with a breeze or burn off with the sun. Those architects wishing to satisfy an existential need to remain close to nature have sought ways to embody these dynamic forces. Rather than merely opening buildings to nature's changing spectacles, a more profound relationship is sought by translating the life force of nature into the mass and space of buildings. Daylight plays a pivotal role in these incarnations, for its oscillations power nature's more tangible changes. Even at a simple, perceptual level, light and shade give to objects a vibrant intensity that the heart and eye grasp in an instant.

The slowly rocking shimmer of water has been of exceptional interest in Finland, perhaps because its landscape is dotted with thousands of lakes, and a culture of water has developed around the sauna and lakeside cabins to which Finns retreat every summer. This association is reflected in the country's creation myths, particularly in the oral poetry of *The Kalevala*, which envisions a world emerging from the primeval sea and the formative acts of a Water-Mother.[15] The land itself has a nascent character, as Sigfried Giedion noted: 'Finland, covered with its network of lakes and forests, suggests in its structure the days of the Creation, when water and earth were first separated.'[16]

VM-Housing, Copenhagen, Denmark, 2005, by PLOT

Light further diffuses into the vapour that is trapped in the hall, producing a faint luminescence similar to the dayglow effects around lakes, so dazzlingly captured in paintings by Akseli Gallen-Kallela (see p. 14) and Albert Edelfelt, where one can barely tell up from down.

Alvar Aalto so often attempted to imbue matter with water's gently moving substance that it forms a central motif in his work. The still tonalities of flat planes are massaged periodically by liquid contours at the Villa Mairea (1941; pp. 104, 132), in Noormarkku, with its sinuous portico, library screens, stair treads and fireplace hollow, and are suggestive of Finland's mythic origins.[17] A shimmer is brought to the mind's eye by the soft hardness, gaining presence from absence.[18] Liquefactions such as these echo the outdoor pool that the house enfolds, suggesting that water lies at its innermost being. But they also hint at feminine creation, recalling the image from *The Kalevala* of a water deity turning her hand to create the seas and 'bring forth the smooth shores'.[19] Expanding on the Villa Mairea's supple hollows are the

The most literal fusion of building and water occurs in the public baths, where people are refreshed in luminous waters that feel as if they are outdoors. Consider Aarne Ervi's Tapiola Swimming Hall (1965), more pavilion than enclosure, its illumination angling in through a glass curtain and raining down from a circular skylight. More evocative is the approach taken by Helin & Siitonen at their Forssa Swimming Hall (1993), where illumination filters through a broken canopy, past columns resting on narrow islands to brighten sheets of glistening water.

their fluid effects into a vertical plane.[20] Aalto went so far as to coat entire façades with this rippling image, carrying its hide-and-seek of light into rooflines that swell and crest like waves – a total conversion of solid matter to liquid light that also characterizes the Seinäjoki Town Hall (1965) and Rovaniemi Theatre (1975), both in Finland. A similar alchemy is performed with detached panes of glass by Lahdelma & Mahlamäki at their Maritime Centre Vellamo (2008), in Kotka, Finland, bringing an effervescence to the rising wave of its overall mass.

Because Aalto's midnight-blue tiles are so dark, we can never fully grasp their surface, but merely catch an elusive glitter, similar to that of a moonlit lake. Flecks of light dance over a surface that has almost disappeared, its depths murky and silent. One senses the last feeble glow of winter night amid tones that congeal and turn black, an experience captured by Finnish poet Bo Carpelan:

> In the November dark the
> water is no longer water
> It moves cold and sluggish
> like black oil,
> sprinkled with broken light.
> It will never be summer
> again.[21]

Another example of the ceaseless energy that underlies nature derives from meteorological phenomena, such as the turbulence of drifting clouds and whorls of mist. Ceilings stirred by wafting light have their own impressive lineage in Nordic architecture, reaching an eloquent peak in the art and architecture of Denmark. The dramatic presence of clouds in a large sky, amplified by the

Säteri Housing, Espoo, Finland, 2002, by Brunow & Maunula

shadow gradations of undulant walls for which Aalto was famous, including the canted waves of timber ribs at the Finnish Pavilion for the 1939 World's Fair, which reappear in smaller form at the Alvar Aalto Museum (1971; p. 79). Some of Aalto's largest petrified waves are shaped with bricks, such as the river-facing curves of the Baker House (1948) at MIT, in Massachusetts, which recalls the sinuous wall of trees around a Finnish lake: a contour with liquid origins.

At times Aalto impressed his watery light more directly into the substance of buildings, but always with sufficient abstraction to touch the soul before the mind. The corridors of the National Pensions Institute (1956; p. 210), in Helsinki, have the ruffled sheen of a glassy lake, stirred by wind. Floors coated with polished strips of alternating black and white marble echo into walls that are ribbed with dark-blue porcelain tile and white mortar, causing the halls to tremble with tiny vibrations. This tonal play on semi-cylindrical tiles, already alive with darting highlights that appear and disappear, is exaggerated by tilting

mild landscape, was of central interest to the nineteenth-century painters Johan Christian Dahl, C. W. Eckersberg and Christen Købke, who kept meteorological diaries. This fascination is echoed in the white vaulting of medieval churches, precursors to Jørn Utzon's church at Bagsværd (1976; p. 56), itself a masterpiece of billowing light and poetically linked to the Danish climate. Externally clad with pale sheets of corrugated asbestos siding, shifting above to glazed tiles and finally to pedimented skylights, the rectilinear mass grows reflective with height to gradually dissolve into the sky. The interior, however, is covered with something ineffable and unexpected: a firmament of sinuous vaults, made to surge and float by on their way to the altar. Utzon's preliminary sketches leave no doubt as to his inspiration; they depict an outdoor scene where voluminous clouds gather over an earthen ground, suggesting a place where the sky has presence and forms a natural ceiling. In one drawing, Utzon abstracts these elements into a building, with the ground now paved and the ceiling a series of curving vaults. Related

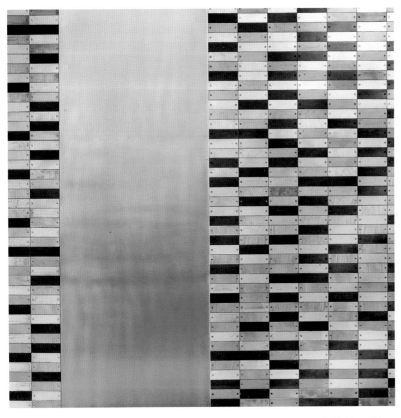

Tapiola Churchyard Urn Cemetery, Espoo, Finland, 2004, by Lahdelma & Mahlamäki

images appear in Aalto's acoustic ceilings, from the wood-lined waves over the lecture hall of the Viipuri Library, to the white waves over his churches at Vuoksenniska (1959; pp. 104, 160) and Seinäjoki (1960; pp. 10, 44), both in Finland, each ostensibly shaped to propagate sound and to create light undulations expressive of the Nordic sky.

One architect who placed his confidence in more earthly forces was Reima Pietilä, to the extent that his buildings have a mineral character comparable to the geology of Finland. Broken facets of walls and roofs, their folds derived from both the immediate site and the glacial terrain, were used to construct a 'morphology of landscape'. This geomorphic language found its most poetic sublimation in Pietilä's Kaleva Church (1966; pp. 98, 170), at Tampere, where light slips through an irregular ring of tall concrete channels to play over the battered texture left by the formwork. Spread over the walls are infinitesimal gradations of light into shadow, and then back into light. The wonderfully shattered,

flashing tones are those we associate with the broken-rock formations of Finland's granite landscape, which, as Pietilä remarked, emerged from the ice only nine thousand years ago. The church's on-and-off beats also imply a more purely fluid energy, creating huge, rolling waves of light, inside of which are tinier waves that advance and recede at a slower pace. Wherever one gazes, rippling tones seize the eye and draw it around a continuous vortex, slightly inflected towards the altar and its backlit sculpture, The Broken Reed. Related migrations occur on the ceiling and along the floor with its wide pews of Finnish pine. These serial motions, reminiscent of Giacomo Balla's Dynamism of a Dog on a Leash (1912) and other Futurist visions, carry a sound analogy for Pietilä, who argued that the tones 'achieve a visual weightlessness by

Dronningegård Housing, Copenhagen, Denmark, 1958, by Fisker, Møller & Kristensen

using rhythmic and light kinetics of broken line chains in constantly evolving series. It is similar to the quick sequences in organ music.'[22]

A somewhat different image appears at the residence for the Finnish president (1993; opposite and p. 12), where Pietilä interlocked granite and glass in a single, geomorphic mass, alive with glinting light. Abstracting the site's granite ridge is a winding series of jigsaw-like walls, which form a base for equally notched and folded glass walls that are brought flush at the roofline to emphasize their earthen bond. The gradation from opaque to transparent gives the building a rockiness and iciness, reminiscent of rock crystal, in which diaphanous prisms emerge from a bed of opaque minerals.[23] The results come close to realizing Bruno Taut's dream of a half-century before: 'Bare grey rock, rising from the green of the forests. Its haphazard shape must be smoothed into angular planes. Crystalline shapes of white glass shimmer in their rocky setting. More such crystals in the depths of the forests.'[24]

If the forces that inspirit nature are independent of outward forms, couldn't they be embodied in architecture without the burden or pre-dictability of metaphor? This prospect is increasingly leading Nordic architects to so thoroughly abstract nature's energy that it becomes effec-tively free of depiction, while still resonating with half-conscious memories. This distillation is usually achieved through the rigour of

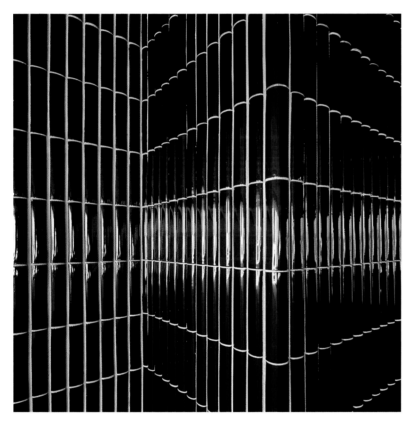

Finlandia Hall, Helsinki, Finland, 1971, by Alvar Aalto

geometry and repetitive texture, reducing undulation to a rhythmic play of points, lines and planes amid simple, Euclidean volumes. An uncom-promising oscillation of this kind, nearly devoid of representational content and sentimentality, identifies many buildings that we instinctively recognize as Scandinavian, from Aalto's fan-shaped theatres and libraries and Fisker, Møller & Kristensen's Dronningegård Housing (1958; oppo-site), to the more decorative skins of Brunow & Maunula's Säteri Housing (2002; p. 47), PLOT's VM-Housing (2005; p. 46), and three buildings by 3XN: the FIH Erhvervsbank (2002), Saxo Bank (2008; p. 50), and

Horten Headquarters (2009; p. 51), all in Copenhagen. In some cases, the light pulsations shrink into fractal-like textures – from the diagonal ribbing of Pietilä's hearth at Mäntyniemi (below) to the small, metal plates of Lahdelma & Mahlamäki's Tapiola Urn Cemetery (2004; oppo-site) and Braille-like cladding of Snøhetta's Oslo Opera House (2008) – causing a new scale of energy to appear at close range, and never die out.

President's Residence, Mäntyniemi, Finland, 1993, by Reima Pietilä

Another vantage point from which to understand the calm, inner ferment of Nordic architecture is provided by artist Per Kirkeby (see p. 7). Conceived as 'light-shadow-machines', Kirkeby's work throws all atten-tion onto mesmerizing tonal rhythms that are built up from dotted and serried patterns, and then made to overlap so that a third pattern emerges. The hypnotic chains of niche and projection, including enfilades within parallel walls through which people may peer and enter, set off an ebb and flow of energy with transparent depths. Austere iterations of direct light and half-light, pellucid shade and black shadows in joints and crevices, recall the hypnotic spaces of Giorgio de Chirico and Louis I. Kahn.[25] Stripped of outward familiarity, these oscillations echo the innermost rhythms of life, and by forever repeating, while still varied in tone, gain a kind of metaphysical weight.

Many Nordic architects have likewise tried to purify their buildings, inside and out, to diverse but unified rhythms of light, whose currents enliven without disturbing an overall stillness. In doing so, stress is placed on a sufficient complexity of scale and overlap so that the building itself is vivified and gives the eye a living experience, thus avoiding the deadening impact of mere repetition. In one of Denmark's greatest works of polyrhythm, the Grundtvigs Church (1940; p. 180) by Peder Vilhelm Jensen-Klint, the pointillist tones of yellow brick and endless replication of empty bays cause the volumes to quietly vibrate in every part, and at every scale. Rather than using a single periodic repetition, two or more rhythms were used simultaneously, which are both nested and overlaid to transform with a person's gaze and distance. Oscillations of light are recursive, and repeat themselves while undergoing change, thereby ranging over many different frequencies without falling into a periodic repetition equated with machines, rather than life.

Rhythmicity at multiple scales brings a never-ending, animate flicker to buildings as dissimilar as Sigurd Lewerentz's twin chapels (1943; p. 101) at Malmö's Eastern Cemetery, in Sweden; Aarno Ruusuvuori's Hyvinkää Church (1961; p. 60), in Finland; Paul Niepoort's Sønderbro Church

Saxo Bank, Copenhagen, Denmark, 2008, by 3XN

(1972), in Denmark; and Sverre Fehn's Aukrust Museum (1996; p. 64), in Norway – all of which are vaguely aroused by a flux that never completely reaches equilibrium, since there is always some irregularity mixed into the regularity. Another marvellous instance of randomness amid order is Peter Celsing's Bank of Sweden (1976; p. 18), in Stockholm, its ponderous mass brought alive by the uneven rhythms of rough-hewn granite and their interplay with other grids in the layered façade. This living pulse returns within the pleated walls and window bays of the light well, whose slender ripples rise unbroken from garden to roof. To vary and naturalize the rhythmic light, Celsing placed in each slender window a potted plant that over time would grow and transform – an idea that is continued into the ceiling, where sun-shading trails of chestnut vine stretch beneath the flutter of skylights.

Carrying these hard-edged abstractions to their ultimate conclusion, refining buildings down to a commingled energy of points, lines and planes of luminous matter, is the architecture of Juha Leiviskä. In his buildings, one can detect images of nature, from stands of trees and serried light to undulations of new-fallen snow or rippling curtains of the aurora borealis, but all these metaphors slip away in the presence of such a basic encounter with the raw energy that inspirits our world. More than all of his colleagues, both Nordic and international, Leiviskä gives compelling expression to our understanding of light as both wave and particle, and the vibrating intensity that stems from a complex interaction of energy and matter. His light also bears a close analogy to sound waves, and music based on lyrical iteration.[26] The reverberant tones that flow through his Church of the Good Shepherd (2002; p. 68), in Finland, possess an astonishing range of scales, all lifted into the air, where they hover in space like a visible form of choral music. Stanzas rise and fall, emerge and disappear, and slide through one another to avoid falling into a tedious pattern. The constant yet soft vibrato of light emerges slowly and then echoes away, flowing up as well as down, and then shifts size while mutating from planes to lines, and then into points. This quivering image, along with many other traits of Nordic light, finds a close analogy in the culture of

Horten Headquarters, Copenhagen, Denmark, 2009, by 3XN

Japan, which is equally based on the truth that life is inherently rhythmic in nature.[27]

Although traditional Japanese villas, tea houses and shrines are the most persuasive manifestation of this wisdom, architects such as Takefumi Aida are using industrial matter and huge, layered walls to create fresh images of embodied energy. But if Aida's resonance is formal and aesthetic in conception, there is clearly a more metaphysical aim to the spell cast by Leiviskä, which produces a sensation equivalent to tremulous sounds. A quiet ripple moves through his churches, with a mystical air that solid form could never express. The whispering tones can be likened to a fugue, or a liturgical chant, where hushed voices blend and echo through the air, using plain vibrations to convey to the senses something of transcendental reality.

ÅRHUS TOWN HALL
ÅRHUS, DENMARK, 1942
BY ARNE JACOBSEN

The misty swirls of grey marble that envelop the exterior of Århus Town Hall give way inside to tighter, more geometric oscillations. Visitors enter via a four-storey hall, lit by a ceiling of frosted glass, its curvature pressing upward as if buoyant with air and complementing a basement stair that coils down into the darkness, dynamically linking earth and sky. This epicentre sets off a chain of pulsations that flow down each of two intersecting wings, echoing the paths of human movement. The large hall to the west plunges out to the city through a huge glass wall, its passage slowed by railings that flicker at three different speeds. Overhead is a gently contoured saw-tooth roof, its mild curves exerting yet another undulation, while flowing by in serial motion and bringing to mind wispy clouds that have been caught on a current of wind. Extending south is the office wing, hollowed along its centreline to illuminate every floor. Falling light accentuates the polyrhythm of brass handrails and other lines, whose luminous beats overlie one another – white columns and beams, balusters and mullions, set against the dottings of lamps and striations of wood.

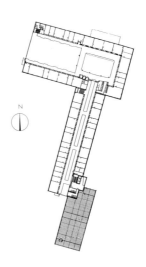

Above Entryway; *top* Partial section of the main hall from the north; *right* Upper-level plan

Upward view from the basement stair in the entry hall

View from the west through the main hall to the entry hall beyond

View across the office wing to the staircase

Office wing with light well at left

Wood slats and concrete structure

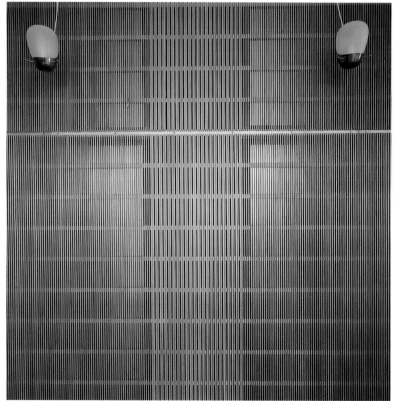

Screen of wood slats

BAGSVÆRD CHURCH
BAGSVÆRD, DENMARK, 1976
BY JØRN UTZON

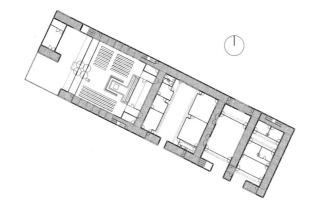

Oscillations coursing through Jørn Utzon's church at Bagsværd culminate in the sanctuary, where white vaults pile up with rays of light that slip between, much as in Denmark's cloudy skies. The wave starts low at the entry, then suddenly rises and breaks momentarily, before climaxing at the point where light is strongest – above the altar – to finally recede in diminishing ripples past the sacristy beyond. The current of energy inflects human movement towards the altar, echoing the churchgoer's journey to Christ. As the most purely luminous elements in the church, the upcurving vaults lift the eye and appear to hover free of the earth, imparting a celestial mood. Emphasizing this levitation is the detachment of vaults by the skylit aisles, where illumination carves away the supporting structure. With light arriving indirectly to the vaults from a single slit window, its shadows are gently drawn out to give the curves a veiled softness. Enhancing this ethereality is the subtle imprint of shuttered concrete, adding faint vibrations to the surface and melting the shadows into a transparent clair-obscure.

Above Detail of the south façade; *top* Plan; *below, left to right* Longitudinal section, looking south; sketch of the vaulting

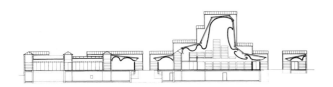

Overall view from the west

Skylit corridor with sun

View of the gallery and staircase to ground level

Skylit corridor surrounding the church

Skylit gallery at upper level

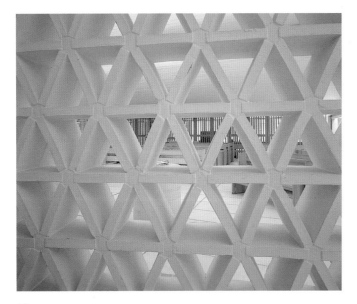

Altar screen

Vaulting at upper level

Detail of the vaults beyond the altar

Vaulting above the altar

HYVINKÄÄ CHURCH
HYVINKÄÄ, FINLAND, 1961
BY AARNO RUUSUVUORI

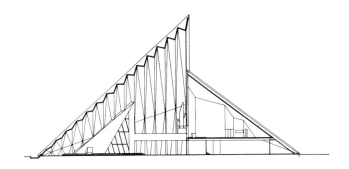

Forming this church at Hyvinkää are two intersecting pyramidal volumes, derived from the image of two hands, folded in prayer, which then reappears at downshifting scales in the altar recess and structural ribs. The ribs are neither uniform nor static, but angled to meet from opposing directions, and taper to points that initiate more ribs beyond. Stemming from the practical needs of structural efficiency, these raised members are lit from one side by the south-facing clerestory, giving each white corrugation one side in light and one in shadow. As a result, the ribs appear to detach from the shell and float in space, but also dissolve into a series of waves that calmly animate the rigid geometry. The ambient flutter resonates into timber pews, and calls attention to the one still point in the church – an evenly lit chancel with a completely silent pool of light.

Above Detail of the sunlit ceiling; *top* Section looking north; *below* Plan

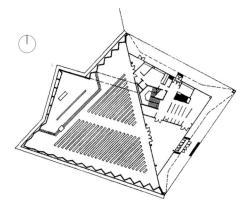

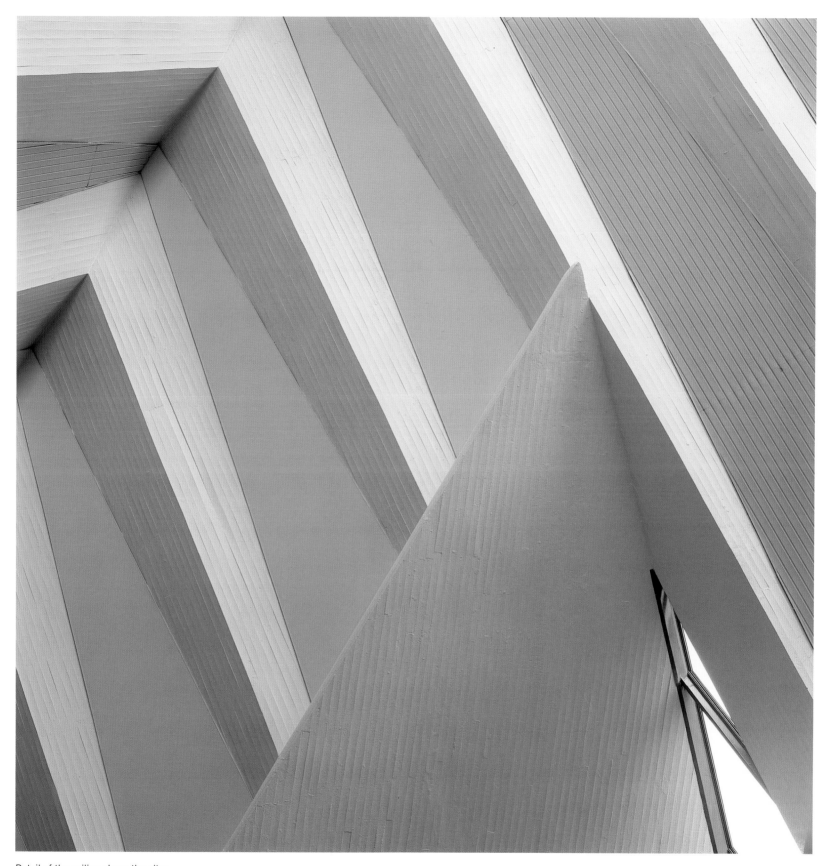

Detail of the ceiling above the altar

Upward view of the ceiling and clerestory

Overall interior view from the east

AUKRUST MUSEUM
ALVDAL, NORWAY, 1996
BY SVERRE FEHN

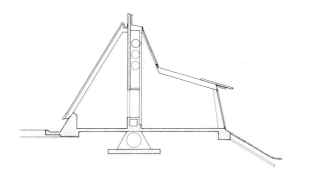

Reduced to a line in the landscape, Sverre Fehn's Aukrust Museum is brought back to life by oscillations that emerge from the earth and guide human movement along an unremitting axis. Extending through the building is a concrete wall, which divides the museum from the administrative offices and brings into distinction two exterior geologic rhythms. Facing south is a steep-pitched roof that is clad with slate, forming a mosaic of dark, mineral light. The north-facing galleries, by contrast, are set on a plinth of loose stones, their peppered tones rising into unmortared walls. The long, glass wall and skylight are, in Fehn's words, 'stretched like a transparent skin' between mountain ranges to the east and west. But this band is induced to vibrate inside by the tight alternation of structural bays. Paralleling the beats of zenithal light, which are produced by tightly spaced concrete members, are the closely matched, but not equal beats of side light, divided by pine columns, which together blend into a polyrhythm of on-and-off pulses that echo human movement from one end of the museum to the other.

Above Detail of the south roof; *top* Transverse section, looking west; *below* Plan

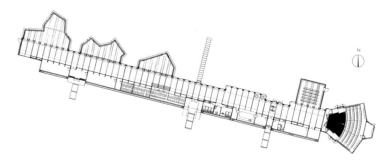

Above View from the west; *top* View from the north

Upward view to the repeating structure and skylights

Underside of the entrance canopy

South wall of the central gallery

Incantation of tremulous tones

CHURCH OF THE GOOD SHEPHERD
PAKILA, FINLAND, 2002
BY JUHA LEIVISKÄ

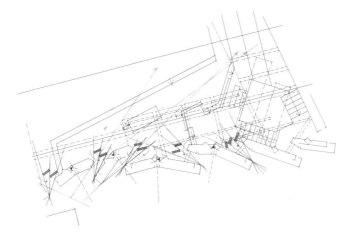

Unlike the huge parallel planes that filter light into Juha Leiviskä's churches at Myyrmäki (1984; p. 22) and Männistö (1992; p. 154), also in Finland, here the altar wall is constructed from layers of slender baffles that quicken and multiply light oscillations. Slight variations in their width, and the degree of twisting with respect to one another, produce a wide range of white tonalities. Each baffle takes a slightly different shade according to the amount of light it receives from behind, complicated by ethereal colours that are cast onto the surface from reflections off concealed paint or wavy refractions from hidden prisms. The sooth-

ing power of this optical flutter depends entirely on the physical blankness and nuanced lighting of the repetitive baffles, whose variation is sufficient to simulate life. 'Uneven reverberations are very human,' Leiviskä has noted, 'for the heart never beats in a mechanical way.' Only by ever-changing iterations can the murmur be rid of both monotony and distraction, or even conscious aesthetic perception. The eye is not bored, but neither is it excited. Instead, it is visually stunned, even anaesthetized, by a wide array of vacant tones left to tingle in the eye. The air itself is made to stir in a hypnotic way, as suspended lamps rise and fall in waves of four, grouped into clusters of golden spots and silvery filaments. As the humming tones urge breath and heart to beat more calmly, our internal rhythms settle down, drawing us into a contemplative mood.

Above Syncopation of natural and artificial light; *top* Plan of the altar wall, with shifting angles of sunlight

Gallery

Overall view of the altar wall from the gallery

Altar wall from the nave

Upward view of the altar wall and ceiling

Detail of the prisms and baffles

Crematorium Chapel, Woodland Cemetery, Sweden, 1940, by Gunnar Asplund

3

JOURNEY

The galvanizing of space with alluring cues and beacons of light

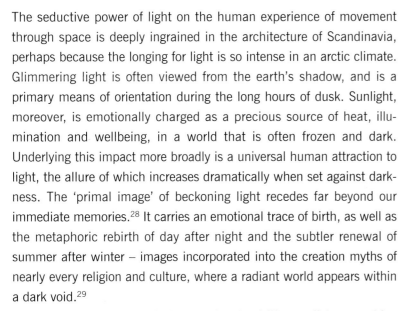

Töölö Branch Library, Helsinki, Finland, 1970, by Aarne Ervi

Main building, Jyväskylä University, Finland, 1959, by Alvar Aalto

The seductive power of light on the human experience of movement through space is deeply ingrained in the architecture of Scandinavia, perhaps because the longing for light is so intense in an arctic climate. Glimmering light is often viewed from the earth's shadow, and is a primary means of orientation during the long hours of dusk. Sunlight, moreover, is emotionally charged as a precious source of heat, illumination and wellbeing, in a world that is often frozen and dark. Underlying this impact more broadly is a universal human attraction to light, the allure of which increases dramatically when set against darkness. The 'primal image' of beckoning light recedes far beyond our immediate memories.[28] It carries an emotional trace of birth, as well as the metaphoric rebirth of day after night and the subtler renewal of summer after winter – images incorporated into the creation myths of nearly every religion and culture, where a radiant world appears within a dark void.[29]

The intimation of beginnings and revived life parallels something more instinctive in nature: the sheer visual magnetism of light fighting off darkness. The rising sun, a fire at night or a lamp in the window is not merely another neutral object in one's visual field, for we hunger for light when it is missing, turn towards its glow when it appears, gaze hypnotically on its emissions, and, when far away, are impelled to gravitate towards its source. Part of this attraction is perceptual, for light

enabled our ancestors to foresee dangers and predators while darkness obscured them, directly affecting human survival over aeons of evolution. But the overwhelming lure of light amid shadows is also due to our basic affinity for the energy and spark of life itself, and equation of light with the promise of existence. 'Within the soul from its primordial beginnings, there has been a desire for light and an irrepressible urge to rise out of the primal darkness,' wrote C. G. Jung in *Memories, Dreams, Reflections*. 'The longing for light is the longing for consciousness.'[30]

Throughout architectural history, the urgent appeal of light against darkness has offered a way to galvanize space by introducing to static volumes an optical charge that attracts attention and stimulates movement. This emotional as well as perceptual force is the determining factor in most architectural narratives, from the spellbinding trail of light along a colonnade to the transcendental glow at the end of a dark nave – as Inger and Johannes Exner made irresistible at their Sankt Clemens Church (1963; opposite), in Randers, Denmark. It is not primarily the quantity of light following darkness that matters in captivating the eye, but rather a quality of light whose powerful character is able to exert a deep hold on the affections of many people, and whose special intensity is woven into a larger sequence that is collectively enthralling and memorable. A major source of the human pleasure in walking through buildings comes from the way that spaces, whether dim or bright, warm

Sankt Clemens Church, Randers, Denmark, 1963, by Inger and Johannes Exner

Mærsk McKinney Møller Institute, Odense, Denmark, 1999, by Henning Larsen

or cool, toplit or sidelit, are composed to play off one another in juxtapositions that elicit feelings of tension and release, gloom and exhilaration, suspense and relaxation, even fear and hope.

In developing processional themes suited and true to their own world, Nordic architects have benefited from the early Modernist *promenades architecturales* of Le Corbusier, along with the American choreographies of Frank Lloyd Wright, whose darkly compressed thresholds and meandering routes were in turn inspired by traditional Japanese houses and temples. But setting apart Scandinavia's narratives is their purity of luminous cues in space, giving them a simple and ageless appeal. Every distraction is stripped away from the surrounding walls, allowing clear outlines and bare reveals to heighten the mesmeric power of light. Where points of light are arranged in series, they offer a chain of beacons to follow, an effect often exploited by Alvar Aalto with skylights in tandem. Positioning a string of luminous cells over a critical path, for instance, allows each in turn to take hold of the eye and pull it along a vector of movement. Aalto's most celebrated sequence is over the main stairway at Jyväskylä University (1959; opposite), its drawing power reinforced by concentrating illumination on the white finishes immediately below, so as to make the entire staircase gleam against neighbouring brickwork.

Other architects have also seized on the primal attraction of serial light in a dark winter climate. Perceptually driving the linear routes

through Sverre Fehn's Norwegian museums are long chains of entrancing skylights, which gently nudge and shepherd visitors from gallery to gallery, a notion applied as well in Henning Larsen's academic buildings, such as the Mærsk McKinney Møller Institute (1999; above), at Odense University. Adding a new twist to this phenomenon is the Exners' Gug Church (1972; pp. 82, 149), at Aalborg, Denmark, where the route to the sanctuary is guided by a sequence of light slots. As churchgoers are drawn along the path to spiritual enlightenment, their journey is broken up into episodes by each new penetration of light. The process of entrance is made more conscious as people arrive many times at the same destination, while impelling them to slow down and become aware of a progressive holiness.

In narratives that are based on movement up or down with respect to the ground plane, darkness below and light above introduce an emotional charge, with cosmic implications. To descend below ground is to enter the earth and undertake a subterranean journey, a realm associated with caverns, tunnels and crypts, but also touched with the irrational forces of fear and myth. One building that is founded on earthen manoeuvres is Timo and Tuomo Suomalainen's Temppeliaukio Church (1969; pp. 76, 81). While not literally descending, the visitor enters by winding through tunnels that have been bored into an outcrop of granite. Light is lost and yearned for as one proceeds down twisting corridors,

Temppeliaukio Church, Helsinki, Finland, 1969, by Timo and Tuomo Suomalainen

Temppeliaukio Church, Helsinki, Finland, 1969, by Timo and Tuomo Suomalainen

feeling along dimly exposed walls of rock, to finally emerge in a large hall that is unaccountably filled with light, which pours through the roof and causes the copper ceiling to glow. This underground passage draws on many primitive images, from the womb to the labyrinth, and the mystery of Paleolithic caves. The ovoid church adds to the impression of having reached a half-buried egg, following a trip through deep, almost uterine slots and trenches. It is remarkable that feelings of this kind can persist even in subterranean spaces that are cleansed by geometry and paint, such as the columbarium located beneath Kristian Gullichsen's Kauniainen Church (1983 and 1998; pp. 78, 106), in Finland. This space of urns is reached by a sloping descent into the earth, marked by the promise of light around a far corner and culminating in a white room that is lit entirely from above. To enter this cavern, one must cross a black stream of water, a Styxian rite in which the darkness and sound and shimmer of water add to the drama of stepping into a catacomb.

For new buildings erected upon the foundations of old structures, descent into darkness and ascent into light are imbued with memories of history. Sverre Fehn's Hedmark Museum (1979 and 2006; p. 86), in Norway, takes full advantage of these associations, giving its routes the feeling of a journey through time. The museum's dim undercroft of archaeological ruins is overlooked by new concrete bridges and ramps, and roofed with a timber-frame structure and skylights, so that visitors

continually weave down to a dark, mysterious past, or up to a brighter and clearer present. Overlaid on the vertical image of earth and sky is an interplay of historic eras, reminding us that the present is built upon the past, but also reflecting the verticality of our own mental structure, where a dark unconscious occasionally rises to enter and disturb conscious thought. At the Rovaniemi Art Museum (1986), in Finland, Juhani Pallasmaa exploited a similar dialectic to avoid civilizing the unconscious, and instead provoke a dramatic tension between cellar and attic, as well as between the irrational and rational.

The vertical sagas of Gunnar Asplund's architecture are outwardly purged of primeval roots, yet deliberately charged between darkness below and the light in an abstract sky above. Particularly impressive is the ritual ascent to the lending hall of Stockholm's City Library (1927; opposite and p. 81). The route begins with a dim, rather tight vestibule, where light is absorbed by facing walls of polished black stucco, carved to catch glints that accentuate their blackness. Springing from this dark compression are shadowy stairs that curve off at either side of the central axis to an upper administrative level, keeping all attention focused ahead on the narrow staircase, which rises towards the beckoning glow of the lending hall and the enlightening power of its books. After squeezing through this passage into raining light, and undergoing a symbolic rebirth, the visitor arrives from below in a great luminous cylinder. The

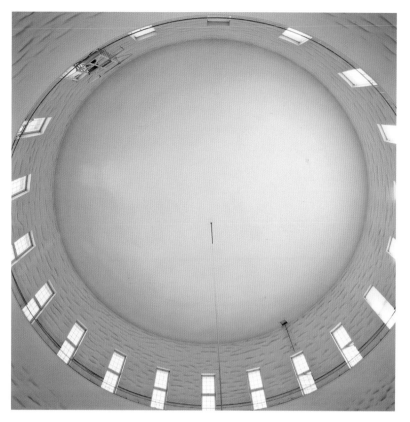

Stockholm City Library, Sweden, 1927, by Gunnar Asplund

Stockholm City Library, Sweden, 1927, by Gunnar Asplund

route does not end, but continues to loop around the drum's base and press upward along the curving stairs and tiers of books. The celestial image of this memorable room derives in part from its circular shape, but also from a vertical contrast of earthy darkness and airy light. While the cylindrical base is lined with wood, forming an uppermost fringe of ground, the glowing white void above is pierced with windows that seem to spin, drawing one's gaze to a limitless space.

In subsequent buildings, Asplund remained fascinated with the aerial psyche, and organized rooms around great stairways that soar into light. This conquest of space is heightened at the Göteborg Law Courts (1937) by etherealizing the means of ascent. The main stair's gentle incline protracts the climb and appears to hover, while the lift has been thinned down to gossamer frames and a glassy shaft. Culminating these routes is a hovering stair that climbs through the ceiling, where it disappears in a void of light – the final ascent to a mystery beyond. By creating both an opposition and means of communication between darkness below and light above, Asplund's stairways give concrete form to our basic realities of earth and sky, and thereby replicate our world, turning climbing into an act that differentiates and unites these polar realms. Superimposed on the lure of light is an experience of freedom and levitation. The source of this human aspiration is the subject of Gaston Bachelard's book *Air and Dreams* (1943), in which he concludes that

the same imaginative operation 'attracts us to both light and height'.[31] The human pleasure of climbing a stair into growing light is permeated with 'oneiric flight' – a wish 'to leave the earth' and 'rise naturally towards the sky, with the wind, with a breath of air, carried directly by our feeling of ineffable happiness'.[32] This timeless joy is repeatedly satisfied in the attic of Peter Celsing's Bank of Sweden (1976; p. 18), in Stockholm, with its skyward release at the top of a dark, geologic building – a celestial space where people are able to lounge and exercise, bathe and dine, amid the passing sun and clouds.

Taking advantage of a hillside site, the ascensional image composed by Heikkinen-Komonen at the Rovaniemi Airport Terminal (1992; p. 81) develops horizontally, rather than vertically. To keep travellers orientated, the dark metal box is opened solely to the runway side, placing a constant temptation of light beyond the shadowy room. Marking out stages along this continuum are walls that decompose into ever-finer screens, their density shifting from rectangular grids to the molecular glow of industrial mesh around the departure lounges. The closer one gets to embarkation, the more the walls melt into light. Complementing this rarefaction is a growing appearance of light underfoot in the highly polished floor, as if the terra firma was being replaced by air and mist. For those who are landing, the process is reversed, but visualized in either direction are the changes of state felt inside. At the final limit before descent

Kauniainen Church & Columbarium, Finland, 1983 and 1998, by Kristian Gullichsen

Kauniainen Church & Columbarium, Finland, 1983 and 1998, by Kristian Gullichsen

to the tarmac, travellers enter a transparent tube just beyond the glazed terminal, suspended in air and hinting at what is to come.

Another genre of ritual motion is the circuitous route, where people advance by circling their destination. In this 'scenario of initiation', to use religious historian Mircea Eliade's phrase, the goal is traditionally bright and the route dark to make the journey a struggle towards light.[33] Aalto reversed this paradigm at the Säynätsalo Town Hall (1952; p. 234), to create a distinctly Nordic mood. Here, the final ascent culminates a series of arrivals that began with the island's shady pine forest, followed by steps that squeeze between heavy, brick masses close to the earth, leading to an outdoor court that frames the sky. Along the way, one seems to be moving ever deeper inside, while rising through diversely lit spaces, which slow down arrival and heighten a sense of growing intimacy. The final climb, slipping up between linings of wall lit from above, has an air of secrecy that is reminiscent of the labyrinthine delay and multiple linings of a castle. One finally emerges into a room from which most illumination is extinguished, a space with a twilit atmosphere. A similar circumambulation around a dark core, while climbing through a shower of light, brings a mythic dimension to Henning Larsen's Ny Carlsberg Glyptotek Addition (1996; p. 92), in Copenhagen.

A special distinction among Scandinavia's processional routes belongs to those that incorporate the landscape, intermingling natural and built episodes of light. These journeys open views to diverting scenery, and employ abstract images of nature to transform our awareness of the world. A persuasive example is Aalto's Villa Mairea (1941; pp. 104, 132), where paths originate in and continually refer back to the wooded terrain. Established at the entrance is a route that meanders like a walk in the woods, expressing a deeply Finnish understanding of place. Past the main doors, the path dims and turns faintly subterranean, making the previous stage 'a sort of porch at the entrance of a burrow', to borrow Henry David Thoreau's words in describing his own hut on Walden Pond.[34] A subsequent rise out of the earth, as if up through the forest floor and into a branching nest, is implied by the rising levels and wrapping of sticks, along with an increasingly luminous floor that shifts from natural flagstones outside to rustic red slate in the entryway and smooth tile on the subsequent level, to eventually arrive at the delicate white beech of the living room. The climb to the bedrooms weaves through dense layers of poles, where light flickers as it does among the trees. For the approach to the lakeside Alvar Aalto Museum (1971; opposite), Aalto shifts the metaphor from forest to water. Tremulous light on the outer tiles facing Lake Päijänne is followed by the smudgy reflections of metal doors, and finally the placid gleam of galleries inside.

Metaphors largely disappear in the intermittent return to nature of Bo & Wohlert's Louisiana Museum of Modern Art (1958; p. 96), in

Resurrection Chapel, Turku, Finland, 1941, by Erik Bryggman

Alvar Aalto Museum, Jyväskylä, Finland, 1971, by Alvar Aalto

Humlebæk, Denmark. Taking this kind of periodicity and tightly compressing it in space and time are the Norwegian narratives developed by Sverre Fehn, each 'an extension of a path in the landscape'. A number of intersecting corridors at Fehn's Villa Busk (1990), in Bamble, Norway, flow out to merge with differing routes in the glacial terrain. About Busk, the architect said: 'I had a feeling of it being a dream about a journey I still had not made.' The itinerary is formed by criss-crossing axes of pulsing light that Fehn calls the 'straight lines of poetry' – a diagonal approach aimed to the hearth and its winter fire, followed by a short cross-axis that culminates in a glass bridge to the children's tower, its line bisected by a sidelit corridor that leads at one end to an indoor pool, and the other to an elevated living room. Glass doors and timber porticoes extend these routes out to nature. And so the entry axis actually originates in a rocky passage under the sky, while the main corridor and its flickering light flows out in one direction along a forest ridge, and in the other climbs a promontory to glimpse the sea.

Fehn's axes of light are most powerfully developed at the Aukrust Museum (1996; p. 64), in Alvdal, and the Aasen Centre (2000) in Ørsta, both in Norway. The spine running through the latter gains narrative power by forming a link between the forest home of the philologist it celebrates and the luminous waters of a distant fjord, tapping into its promise of contact with an outer world. Along this line the visitor encoun-

ters a diverse alternation of light and dark galleries, which multiply events and make the journey feel much longer than it really is. Visitors are also exposed to a repeating geometry that is continually upset and overridden by uneven distributions of light, expressing contemporary ideas about a kind of order that includes disorder. The concrete structure may be periodic, but its illumination, which varies in amount and quality, as well as the angle of its source, is not. Instead of glorifying exactitude and mathematical repetition, the luminous rhythms display syncopation. Long pauses and shifted accents infuse the axis with unpredictability and surprise – an effect that is liberating for the experience of artefacts, but also constructs an analogy to nature that is alive and changing, and resistant to the fixity of death.

To pick up once more on Gunnar Asplund's choreography, a remarkable feature of his two chapels at Stockholm's Woodland Cemetery is their employment of nature to form resurrective scenarios of 'light after darkness'. This message is plainly evident in his early forest chapel (1920), whose huge, hipped roof is sheltered in spruces and clad with dark shingles, looming massive and black over the portico below. But appearing beneath and fighting off darkness is the inviting white gleam of columns and ceiling, an after-image of the dark tree trunks and woodland canopy. Culminating the transfiguration is a toplit white room, a luminous cave within a dark mountain, as well as a cupola that vaults overhead as an abstract sky. In this short but dramatic procession, Asplund employed familiar images drawn from nature to give added meaning to the psychology of bereavement, using analogies of light and darkness to bring comfort to the funeral rite. Seen through this larger prism, the fading and returning light helps mourners come to terms with their loss, rather than deny that loss by disguising the reality of death.

For Asplund's later Crematorium Chapel (1940; p. 72), also at the Woodland Cemetery, the architect expanded this image into a vast composition of earth, forest and sky. The route begins from far away, emerging from the trees and proceeding up a grassy incline that seems to flow into the sky. Several tonal contrasts lure the eye and guide movement: first, a concave horizon of earth and trees that frames the sky at the peak of the hill and the clouds piling up there; followed by a huge, granite cross that breaks the horizon to unite earth and heavens; and finally a loggia that signals arrival. But the journey is not over, for the previous sequence repeats in more compact and abstract form within the loggia. Eyes are drawn to a pool of light that falls into the shade, followed by a sheet of illumination that has slipped through a crevice between anteroom and chapel, and finally latch onto a glass screen that mirrors the panorama behind. Beyond their ability to emotionally charge and guide the way to the chapel, while conveying something of ultimate reality, Asplund's images of 'darkness to light' protract the journey and insert moments of contemplation before a person must gather the courage to enter the womb-like chamber and its rituals.

Another elegy of light, Erik Bryggman's Resurrection Chapel (1941; p. 79), in Turku, Finland, was completed a year after Asplund's chapel. Here, Bryggman presents a series of encounters with reviving light that constitute what is arguably the greatest and most touching narrative space in Scandinavia. The recurring theme of loss and recovery begins with a walk through shadowy forest, leading up to a pale chapel where visitors encounter a dusky portico, a second journey through darkness. Just as one is about to enter a realm where the dead and living coexist, gloomy doors of weathered bronze appear in a glory of decay, a moving expression of old age. Yet here again something new flickers out of death, for the door pulls are covered with small, reflective brass appliqués of growing plants. The pitch-black vestibule that follows, faintly lit by metal globes that have been pierced to glitter like stars at night, interjects a final passage rite between outside and inside – a lonely place the bereaved must cross. Just as light is swallowed by darkness, the luminous chapel is glimpsed beyond through an ironwork screen with silhouettes of winding vines, once more overlaying death with the smile of life. One is suspended for a moment in space and time, like the icy hour before dawn, or womb at birth. Upon emerging into Bryggman's chapel, the visitor beholds a strange ambiguity. The interior is warmly enclosed like a cave, yet flows into the forest at the right, combining

dark protection with an outward lure that repeats in the portico to the graveyard for the coffin. At the same time, attention is drawn past the coffin to the altar wall, where rising vines reach for the sky and its slanting light, implying a celestial journey for the soul. The result is a distinctly Finnish blend of Christianity and Pantheism. To one side is the light of the forest, which belongs to nature and bathes the ground where the dead are buried, and ahead lies a mysterious glow behind the altar, as if sent from heaven. Pews are angled to mingle these feelings, enticing the bereaved to reflect upon life's final journey, and eternity itself.

A more modest example of spiritual rebirth, experienced through images of nature, is Kaija and Heikki Sirén's Student Chapel (1957; p. 136), in Otaniemi, Finland. The route winds through a shady forest, its air scented with pine, followed by a succession of rooms with contrasting moods. First is a forecourt, enclosed by a fence that receives the sky like a forest clearing, followed by a dark vestibule that blots out what has been to clear the heart for what is to follow. Forest light returns in the sanctuary, arriving from two different directions and without any hint of the supernatural. Attention is fixed on the glass altar wall, which makes the landscape part of the chapel and allows those seated in prayer to gaze onto shimmering pines and a white cross outside, exposed to weather.[35] This series of encounters is a clear expression of Mircea Eliade's 'ritual death', followed by a 'mystical rebirth', but instead of transporting people to the supernatural kingdom of God, as the Christian church has attempted since its origins, this thoroughly Nordic chapel invokes heaven on earth. The faithful are shown what is holy in simple stones, trees and light, paralleling the efforts of the plein-air painters a century before, who were equally drawn to the transcendental powers of nature.

Airport Terminal, Rovaniemi, Finland, 1992, by Heikkinen-Komonen

Stockholm City Library, Sweden, 1927, by Gunnar Asplund

Temppeliaukio Church, Helsinki, Finland, 1969, by Timo and Tuomo Suomalainen

Nave from the south, towards the altar

GUG CHURCH
AALBORG, DENMARK, 1972
BY INGER AND JOHANNES EXNER

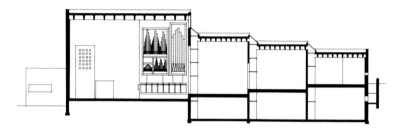

The spiritual journey at this church is structured and guided by a series of light slots. Hints of these segments appear outside as glass strips that divide concrete boxes, stepping up to the church itself. Derived from functional zones that can be closed off or joined to the main hall, the layers of space also give a ritual character to the side corridor, which leads to the sanctuary. Paralleling the rising ceiling are downward slopes in the floor, with each dim ramp beginning and ending in a curtain of light. The theme of tonal subdivision extends into the hatched texture of poured concrete and concrete panels, divided by shadowy joints, as well as a ceiling structure where the grey concrete beams alternate with white infill, causing every part of the building to pulse in sequence towards the altar. As if passing through multiple gates, the visitor encounters stages of arrival that eventually converge on a dark portal, a final threshold that opens onto a climactic pool of light at the altar.

Above Overall view from the west (with later parish addition on the right); *top* Section looking east; *left* Plan

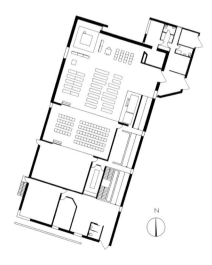

Nave from the north

Church skylights and ceiling

First landing of the corridor to the church

View from the church of the corridor

View from midpoint of the corridor to the entry hall

Journeys through time

HEDMARK MUSEUM
HAMAR, NORWAY, 1979 & 2006
BY SVERRE FEHN

Conceived as a network of paths along ramps and bridges, the museum rewards the moving eye with a series of shifting vantage points from which to gaze upon artefacts and half-excavated ruins. Counterpointing the pace of exhibits, described by the architect as 'the dance of dead things', are contrasting speeds of spatial progression, defined by light: the periodic rain of illumination from glass tiles in the roof; a more rapid flicker of warmly lit spots and lines in the timber framing; and the infrequent but entrancing sidelight from jagged rents or deep windows in the old stone walls. Underfoot is a grey foundation of old stone or new concrete, making the lower galleries earthy and dim, while the upper galleries, which include three small vertical rooms lit from above that house the most delicate objects, are attic-like. The experience of travel through a layered archaeology goes well beyond the reach of the physical eye, for it wanders in and out of a poetical landscape with memories of different epochs of history, all the while weaving down to a dark, subterranean realm and up to a light-filled aerie – a movement that integrates the remarkable tension between two primitive situations.

Ramped passage through light and shadow

Staircase to the upper level of the north wing

Window exhibit

Glimpse through an old wall
in the west wing

View from the bridge into one of the toplit galleries

Paths over ruins beneath the new roof structure

View into one of the toplit galleries in the west wing

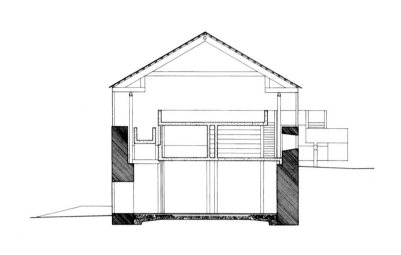

Transverse section of the north wing

Bridge over the excavation zone in the west wing

Ramp to the upper-level galleries of the north wing

Top Roof terrace

Above, left to right Route at left to the French collection and the staircase; landing at the middle-gallery level; flight of steps to the upper-gallery level; view from the lower-gallery level across to the gallery arcade

Helical movement from earth to sky

NY CARLSBERG GLYPTOTEK ADDITION
COPENHAGEN, DENMARK, 1996
BY HENNING LARSEN

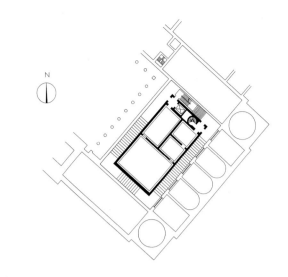

At this addition for an art museum, a toplit stairway wraps around and links the floors of a dark core containing the French collection. By tapering the pylon of galleries, the architect gave the slow ascent and its spatial funnel a mounting sensation of freedom and brightness. Cutting off light to protect the collection's paintings, the central mass suggests a shrine that visitors must circumambulate and enter from various points on the incline. The coil of movement actually winds in two directions, with its lower end sinking below ground and the other rising into the sky. Near the foot of the spiral is a staired descent to the appropriately dim and tomb-like rooms of the Egyptian gallery. From out of this underworld, and its evocation of a distant past, the journey climbs through a growing shower of Danish light. In linking the dim gallery levels, the winding route produces an alternation of light and darkness, extrovert and introvert space, culminating in a roof terrace that takes the entire sky for its ceiling.

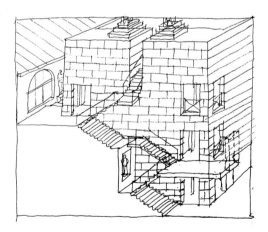

Above View to the staircase, with pylon of galleries at far left; *top* Upper-level plan; *left* Axonometric sketch

Corner of skylight over the staircase

Stair to the roof terrace

Top Continuation of the passage past the Giacometti gallery

Above, left to right Two-storey gallery, with glass wall facing the inland lake; sculptures by Alberto Giacometti under the circular skylight, overlooking the two-storey gallery; initial toplit and sidelit gallery in the north wing; gallery with double-clerestory and high windows

LOUISIANA MUSEUM OF MODERN ART
HUMLEBÆK, DENMARK, 1958
BY BO & WOHLERT

Strung along the coast of Zealand, in eastern Denmark, this museum's detached exhibition halls in the north wing are connected by transparent corridors that make the most of the shifting vistas of inland forest and seaside bluffs. Distinguishing each gallery is a different character of illumination, whose sources range from skylights to clerestories and glass walls along one or both sides. Thus a stroll through the complex involves an episodic series of half-lit galleries of varying atmosphere, each of which is approached and succeeded by a luminous corridor that opens onto changing moods in the neighbouring landscape. Instead of darkness preparing for light, the opposite occurs: bright interludes calm the mind and cleanse the eye as a means to sharpen one's awareness for each new encounter with modern art. The Japanese inspiration for this scenario is not merely one of form and material, for the museum also draws upon the open porticoes that link the gardens and dark interiors scattered around Zen temple compounds, as well as the 'white dewy path' that precedes a tea house – all of whose roles are to soothe the soul and help one to withdraw from everyday tensions, thereby increasing consciousness in preparation for enlightenment, an aim no less relevant to an art museum.

Above Looking back from the zig-zag shift in the glazed corridor; *top* Site plan with the original north wing and later south extension

Kaleva Church, Tampere, Finland, 1966, by Reima Pietilä

4
CARVING

The moulding of light into empty yet compelling and unforgettable figures

In *Colour and Form* (1937), British art critic Adrian Stokes identified two traditions in art that could also be considered approaches to light: 'carving', which produces a sharply defined and self-sufficient object, and 'modelling', which necessitates a more enveloping relationship.[36] In its management of diffuse Northern light, the architecture of Scandinavia has been inclined to epitomize the latter. But coexisting with this predilection, and its dissolution of figure and ground, is the less frequent if still accomplished practice of sculpting light into recognizable and memorable shapes that possess a figural presence.

Where carved light appears in Scandinavian architecture of the past century, it ranges from small but riveting details to monumental light-catching scoops. While the wish to give palpable form to ethereal light

instantaneous pleasure to the eye. When sufficiently arresting, the glowing void displays, in Stokes's words, an open 'face', charged with its own energy and tension and radiating a 'miraculous sensation of fullness'.[37] It stands in space and exists in the true sense of the word, vibrantly there with its own being and invitation to touch.

For those applying classical instincts to luminous figures, such as C. F. Hansen in Denmark, Carl Ludvig Engel in Finland, and Gunnar Asplund and Carl Nyrén in Sweden, the results are perfectly lucid but often rigidly geometric, and at times complacently dull or decorative. A stark contrast can be seen in Alvar Aalto's approach to figural light from the 1930s onwards, in which anonymous yet insistent cavities were employed to shift awareness away from aesthetics and onto light's power

Pieksämäki Cultural Centre, Finland, 1989, by Kristian Gullichsen

Academic Bookshop, Helsinki, Finland, 1969, by Alvar Aalto

is universal and appears throughout architectural history, its Nordic expression tends to favour austerely simple volumes. It is precisely these vacant gestures that allow carved light to harmonize with an ambience of blurry moods, offering yet another means by which to identify with the North. The Scandinavian art of moulding light, however, involves more than reduction to neutral gestalts. The silhouettes of luminous voids, such as windows and skylights, are endowed with distinct and unforgettable shapes, even as they are totally emptied. Their clear and concentrated outlines are able to captivate with a single glance, and give

to transform and invigorate, rather than ornament, physical matter. Among Aalto's subtle achievements in this regard are conical skylights and light-catching scoops that seem carved as much by natural forces as by the architect's hand, for they are hewn in response to geographic realities and the course of the sun. Further reducing aesthetic arbitrariness is an elemental presence of luminous shapes, making them appear neither new nor novel, but beautifully timeless and universal. Many of Aalto's finest rooms, even entire buildings, are experienced through these glowingly vacant, instantly recognizable volumes. But Aalto was equally fond of shrinking this language into details with a powerful character, as in the fireplace carving at Villa Mairea (1941; pp. 104, 132), or the sinuous bulge of the pulpit wall at Vuoksenniska Church (1959; pp. 104, 160), both in Finland, whose mesmerizing profiles push the analogy between architecture and nature beyond traditional limits.

Where classical urges occur in the early buildings of Sigurd Lewerentz, they are overshadowed by mysterious moods where enigmatic shapes of light exert a strange, metamorphic power. Looming over his eerie Resurrection Chapel (1925; p. 177), at the Woodland Cemetery in Stockholm, is a single, bracketed window, whose emanation has a physical vitality that seems to press forcibly into the room. Analogous but cleanly cut voids in Lewerentz's Malmö chapels, including St Gertrude

withholds views of the Mediterranean during entry, allowing only a seductive glimpse though a small crescent window as the front door is opened. This lunar hint conveys that nature is about to be experienced at a more profound level than normal, blending enchantment with cosmic awe – an idea that culminates in the living room, where windows with deeply bevelled reveals trap light, while directing attention to the sea though a series of luminous frames.[38] The masses of light and radiant scenes in these sandstone voids are undiminished by the window frames, which are hidden from sight on the outer wall. When the same plasticity appears in Utzon's roofs, to disseminate light while crowning rooms with distinctive funnels, as in his Herning school prototypes (1970) or the Utzon Centre (2008), designed by the architect with his son Kim, it

Chapel of Hope, Eastern Cemetery, Malmö, Sweden, 1956, by Sigurd Lewerentz

St Gertrude Chapel, Eastern Cemetery, Malmö, Sweden, 1943, by Sigurd Lewerentz

(1943; above, right) and the Chapel of Hope (1956; above), and his later churches of St Mark (1960) at Björkhagen and St Peter (1966; p. 238) at Klippan, both in Sweden, are reduced instead to barren cells in thick walls, their haunting presence arising from absence. Where brickwork folds into window reveals, light appears to eat through the shell and dwell in its corpus, producing a virtual transfiguration.

Certain openings in Jørn Utzon's buildings are sculpted into chambers of light, often as windows that frame radiant views. Set at the edge of a precipitous cliff, his own home Can Lis (1972; p. 102), in Mallorca,

clearly involves the Nordic adaptation of an ancient idea. Behaving as 'natural light fixtures', to employ Louis I. Kahn's term, the skylights form a hollow ceiling that is pregnant with light, a trait also explored by Klas Anshelm at the Malmö Konsthall (1976; p. 214) and Reima Pietilä at the Kaleva Church (1966; pp. 98, 170), in Tampere.

Luminous holes are imbued with stories of bygone days in Sverre Fehn's Hedmark Museum (1979 and 2006; p. 86), at Hamar, Norway. Embrasures in walls of the nineteenth-century farm structure, some painted white to amplify their brilliance, provide miniature galleries for backlit artefacts. In the older, more battered medieval foundations, the ruptures of age are neither filled nor disguised, but instead are gently covered with unframed glass. A different tactic occurs at Fehn's Villa Busk (1990), also in Norway, where windows are distinctly outlined but fused into hybrid figures. A horizontal slot between the wall and roof merges with periodic vertical cuts, to afford a wide panorama of the tree-tops and glimpses of the valley below. Lined with wood to strengthen their silhouettes, these distinctly modern windows vacillate between alternate readings and latent shapes of light. Fehn's moulding of the windows into visual fields concludes at the hearth, where a wood-lined cavity segues down to a white marble slab with its own blue window that adjoins the fire, setting up a tense interplay of warm and cool light.

accents to principal points in space. At the same time, the blank wall or ceiling forms a ground that is punctured or gouged to vivify its plane with faintly anthropomorphic patterns. These lucid yet enigmatic voids turn the plane into a mask, implying a borderline realm that vacillates between logical thought and the sheer delight of human play.

Carved light offers Gullichsen an extra dimension in which to question the solid reality of architecture. Our understanding of the building as an 'object' is challenged, since the most palpable 'thingness' is made from nothingness. In this ambiguous state, figure and ground begin to interchange. Gullichsen's insistence on giving the strongest gestalts to light, rather than solid form, reasserts light's capacity to exist in its own right, apart from its role as illuminant. An analogous impulse to sculpt

Can Lis, Mallorca, Spain, 1972, by Jørn Utzon

Mortuary Chapel, Asker, Norway, 2000, by Carl-Viggo Hølmebakk

Deceptively simple luminous voids act as beacons in Carl-Viggo Hølmebakk's Mortuary Chapel (2000; above, right), beginning with less emphatic shapes in the outer gate and ending with a ritual carving that points the dead to the chapel's true climax – the heavens above. Similar powers of figural light to focus space, while, paradoxically, transforming it into a field of action, take centre stage in the buildings of Kristian Gullichsen, often displaying a mischievous side. At his Kauniainen Church (1983; pp. 78, 106) and the Pieksämäki Cultural Centre (1989; p. 100), both in Finland, glowing cavities serve as circulation cues or

light directly, and hang its shapes on a nondescript ground, is seen in the art of James Turrell, notably his installations *Projection Pieces*, *Wedgeworks* and *Skyspaces*. Turrell has stated that his central aim 'in the perception of light', which could be applied equally to Gullichsen, 'is in giving it thingness. It exists just as a physical object has presence. I make thingness of perception by putting limits on it in a formal manner. There is no object there, only objectified perception. By putting into question physicality and objectness, the work may reveal more about physicality than any physical object.'[39]

Light chambers in Jokela & Kareoja's Hämeenkylä Church (1993; p. 110) at Vantaa, Finland, derive as much from layering as from outlining, as if peeling away various strata within the depth of the shell. Facing the congregation is an altar wall, filled with punctures, whose external openings are hidden behind the foreground layer, producing what the architects call a 'transparent concrete wall', able to 'live with the light.'[40] The wall is actually constructed from two detached linings, with the outer canted to leave a residual space between the two through which light may travel. Openings in each layer are offset to make the cavities glow without any detectable source. 'There is something behind the wall,' Olli-Pekka Jokela explains, 'but nobody knows what it is. When there are services going on in the morning, with sun shining on the wall, and a cloud goes by, it dims the surface and makes it different. All the children stop talking to each other. You know it is a cloud, but...'.[41]

The simplest form of carved light is the linear slit, whose discreet austerity is well suited to the Nordic instinct for restraint. The anonymous yet enigmatic presence of luminous cuts forms a central theme in Lewerentz's Malmö chapels, where incisions were grouped to ooze light and identify thresholds. At St Peter's Church, the slits are fewer, but have been enlarged and are more conspicuous. Placed in the ceiling, rather than wall, at times to guide ritual movement, the cracks are in fact slender volumes extruded into chimney-like shafts that mark without brightening the intentionally dark interior. Reflecting the gravitas of their setting, the repeated twin slots of Arne Jacobsen's National Bank of Denmark (1971; p. 184) dominate the room they tower over. By contrast, the playful slits with which Gullichsen carves ceiling and wall at once, or that relieve enclosure in Käpy and Simo Paavilainens' Finnish churches, such as Olari (1981; pp. 2, 218) and St Michael (1988; p. 112), are less solemn and more transparent to colourful slivers of tree and sky. These slits are not ornamental, however, for they are rid of aesthetic manipulation and seem etched by the penetrating force of light, which optically consumes their contours and implies a corrosive power at work. The Paavilainens often extend this theme into sculptural troughs, whose luminous voids erode and free the edges of ceilings.

Where sliced through the entire envelope to divide a room into segments, radiant lines gain a third dimension and, more importantly, define a new kind of space with their tracery of energy. This phenomenon is a controlling presence in Lund & Slaatto's St Magnus Church (1988; p. 116), in Lillestrøm, Norway. Dissecting the shell with surgical precision, the parallel cuts share an unexpected resemblance to the 'pregnant voids' made in obsolete buildings by American artist Gordon Matta-Clark. In *Splitting* (1974), a series of temporary incursions into houses slated for demolition, Matta-Clark used a power saw to cut the building in half with a continuous crack, pierced by a narrow band of light. 'The cut', he says, 'is very analytical. It's the probe! It was kind of the thin edge of

what was being seen that interested me as much, if not more, than the views that were being created.'[42] In other works, such as *Day's End* (1975), Matta-Clark positioned his cut to direct inside a moving sunbeam, where 'the slit is in fact a zenith point ... a slit across the sun's declination'.[43] A similar experience occurs at St Magnus, where slits admit parallel sunbeams that move in unison over pews and floor. Attention is pulled away from the container and onto a purely perceptual space woven by light, bearing a likeness as well to the 'light lattices' and 'ropes of light' conceived by Japanese architect Shoei Yoh in the 1980s.

Though inscribed by the sky, the cosmic slice through the roof of the Rovaniemi Airport Terminal (1992; p. 81), in Finland, by Heikkinen-Komonen depends more on imagination than vision. As the arrival place for a city renowned for its location on the Arctic Circle, the building commemorates this continuously moving line with an incision – a diagonal cut placed over arriving and departing passengers – which marks the circle's position at the time of the building's construction. In subsequent buildings, the firm expanded the streak of light into an axial channel to orientate people and link the innermost rooms with nature. The boldest of these is the toplit corridor that runs through their Emergency Services College (1992) in Kuopio, its radiant slot extending over 200m and maintained at night by a 'lighting beam' set over the skylight. Echoing this line is a long, glass bridge that connects the training centre to a classroom block. Glazed on three sides with a grate for the floor, the passage demands a sudden attunement to ambient weather, including blanketing fog and winter storms, calling into play perceptual shifts that exercise the agility of emergency personnel.

The glass bridge brings us to an entirely different mode of carved light: the sensuous shaping of glass and its optical properties. The far-reaching effect of industrial glass on modern architecture, and of the glass culture envisioned at the outset of the twentieth century by Bruno Taut, Paul Scheerbart and other members of the Glass Chain, took a unique twist in Scandinavia. Climatic constraints and long winters, which restricted the size of windows, encouraged innovation with small but expressive volumes of glass. Paralleling and often prompting these diaphanous figures is a rich tradition of glass art, especially in Finland, from Aalto's sinuous vases to the primeval works of Timo Sarpaneva, not to mention the geometric elegance of Tapio Wirkkala's tumblers or radiant calm of Kaj Franck's thin glasswork, whose physical substance is reduced to almost nothing.

Another source of the fascination with crystalline matter is a cultural affinity for one of the Arctic's most bewitching phenomena: the pellucid ice that appears in abundance every winter. This entrancing substance is a focus of Tarjei Vesaas's novel *The Ice Palace*, whose main character, eleven-year-old Unn, is spellbound by a hollow ice structure that has formed around a waterfall. 'An enchanted world of small pinnacles, gables, frosted domes, soft curves and confused tracery,' Vesaas wrote. 'Everything shone. The sun had not yet come, but it shone ice-blue and green of itself … the daylight sidled in, glimmering curiously through the ice walls. … Its rays penetrated thick ice walls and corners and fissures, and broke the light into wonderful patterns and colours. … Unn had lost all ties with everything but light.'[44] Translucid ice was also admired by the plein-air painters, who made it a principal subject of winter pictures. Among these is Akseli Gallen-Kallela's *Winter Scene from Imatra* (1893), which portrays a world of ice that is chilled by the vapour of freezing air, and bathed in a cold, green light.

Aalto was quick to grasp the latent poetry of glass in an arctic climate. In a few remarkable glazed openings, especially curvaceous

gazing into and through a solid, transparent body. As we move past these faceted windows, a wonderful shimmer dances before our eyes.

Equally enthralling is the cold, glacial presence of Aalto's 'crystal skylights', as seen in two buildings in Helsinki. Each tented prism above the main hall of the National Pensions Institute (1956; p. 210) is doubled, with one nested inside another, producing a mysterious glitter as the rays play over contrasting slopes. This ricocheted light recalls a Scheerbartian fantasy of the kind described in *Glasarchitektur* (1914) – a realm of 'sparkling jewels' that culminates in the 'enamels' and 'mother-of-pearl coat' of the building's corridors.[45] Closely related in optic behaviour are the three glass lanterns that illuminate the Academic Bookshop (1969; p. 100). Each polygonal lattice is made from panes

Villa Mairea, Noormarkku, Finland, 1941, by Alvar Aalto

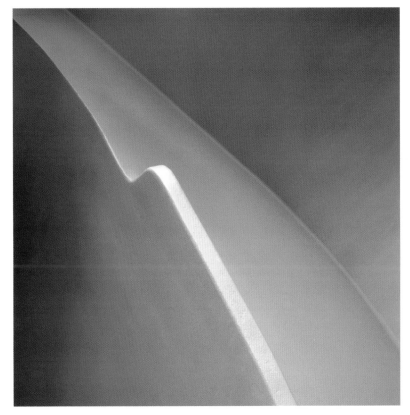

Vuoksenniska Church, Imatra, Finland, 1959, by Alvar Aalto

windows and prismatic skylights, he drew directly on his background in glassware. These transparent forms went beyond practical necessity to express an identity that stemmed from nature. Greeting visitors at his Paimio Sanatorium (1933; p. 21), in Finland, is an undulant curtain of glass, as softly folded as a Savoy vase and lit from above, as well as from the side. A more faceted sparkle appears in the three east windows of Vuoksenniska Church, each consisting of two separate layers that are folded in plan and take contrasting inclines. Scintillation is amplified by overlapping reflections in the tilted panes, making it seem as if one is

that meet at various angles, and is set into a ceiling recess so that it stands in space, as well as contains space. Beyond their pragmatic value in catching and spreading precious daylight, the cells turn radiant by bouncing around the passing rays, appearing white or grey, blue or yellow, according to the weather outside. Making light solid by different means is the snaking glass tube that guides people and scenes around a 90° turn into Jacobsen's National Bank of Denmark. Set against dim grey walls, this double curve takes on a voluptuous presence. Enhancing the shimmer are flickering images of passers-by and the city at large that are caught, distorted and suspended in the curling glass – a periscopic reach with surveillance implications.

Working along an opposite vein are architects who seek to completely eliminate the plasticity of glass, compressing it into weightless sheets that exude their own optical magic. Sigurd Lewerentz, a leading exponent of this reduction, intensified the presence of his unframed windows by setting them against dark masonry at his churches at Björkhagen and Klippan, and against the grey concrete of his Flower Kiosk (1969; below), at Malmö's Eastern Cemetery, while emphasizing their filminess with steel-clipped panes that project from walls by their own thickness. Kept utterly free of the gritty backdrops, these smooth sheets possess a shallow but concentrated self-assurance, like a series of paintings hung

sheets overlap stonework to initiate a dialogue of transparent and opaque, smooth and rough, geometric and irregular, open and solid, new and old. The gossamer films seem almost to float, while splicing back into the world with refracted and reflected images. This dialectic continues into the display cases Fehn designed for various museums in Norway, including the Aasen Centre (2000), in Ørsta, and the Aukrust Museum (1996; p. 64), in Alvdal, whose airy panes form a miniature crystalline architecture. Intersecting sheets held in place by dark steel clips are unrelated to the hermetic cases common to museums, forming instead small glass pavilions that shelter without isolating artefacts. Objects are able to breathe, while their shimmering envelopes engage the eye without overshadowing the exhibits. Free edges and angled faces

Flower Kiosk, Eastern Cemetery, Malmö, Sweden, 1969, by Sigurd Lewerentz

on a wall. As the shimmering plates float against a neutral backdrop, they appear outlined in silver and perceptually advance beyond their actual physical depth, while at the same time isolating fragments of nature into images that are vibrant with energy – to the point where the window ceases to be inanimate.

Picking up the same line of thought, Sverre Fehn placed sheets of frameless glass over the fissures in old stone walls at the Hedmark Museum. But Fehn's glass reaches well past its openings, and is devoid of any sealant that might fuse together window and wall. Instead, the

overlay the objects with a Cubist collage that exists and moves free of them. The transparent sparkle mediates between art and setting, fusing together the scrutiny of things with intriguing reflections of distant space. As the objects are permeated by elusive images that shift with a viewer's angle of sight, they lose their curatorial certainty and objecthood. This shifting perspective admits several vanishing points at once, so as to scramble space and upset its fixed dimensions, an experience that challenges our normal three dimensions of space – a contemporary task still in its architectural infancy.

KAUNIAINEN CHURCH & COLUMBARIUM
KAUNIAINEN, FINLAND, 1983 & 1998
BY KRISTIAN GULLICHSEN

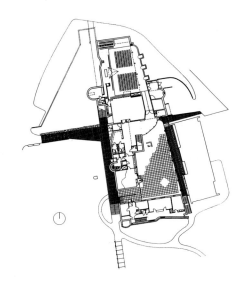

A variety of small, radiant figures, distinct in character, appear and guide the circuitous path into the church. The first superbly concrete images are three glowing voids that beckon beyond a dark, sloping tunnel. Formed at the base of the light shafts, and carved from the seam between ceiling and wall, each profile combines in a playful manner a semicircle above and rectangle below, so as to appear not flat but folded. Upon arriving in the sanctuary, other glowing shapes emerge to identify different activities in space, while evenly illuminating the room – each a near-solid entity that is clearly distinguished from the nondescript walls and ceiling. As a result, the third dimension is sensed less by enclosing planes than by constellations of luminous units. Among these are a triangular roof light over the altar, a row of square holes to mark the pulpit and a vertical slit of coloured glass that points down to the baptismal font. The columbarium is also identified by strongly moulded volumes of light – a series of shafts whose radiant voids rivet attention on the mortuary wall, and exaggerate its urn niches with a vibrant play of light and shade.

Above View of the altar wall from the east; *top* Plan; *below* Longitudinal section, looking west

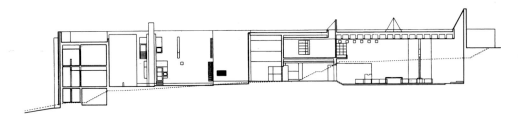

Urn niches below the lightwell in the columbarium

Slit above the baptismal font

Light chute

Arrival into the church at the end of the ramp, with light chutes at the right

Square openings over the pulpit, with window to the parish at left

Triangular skylight above the altar

Corner skylight

HÄMEENKYLÄ CHURCH
VANTAA, FINLAND, 1993
BY JOKELA & KAREOJA

Conceptually tied to the sourceless light of late Baroque churches, especially the illusionistic vaults of Bernardo Vittone, the altar wall at Hämeenkylä is carved into layers to frame a mysterious glow beyond. As with its predecessors, the double-shell works as a plenum that diverts light through an elaborate geometry of luminous cells, meant to bewitch the eye and transcend the normal limits of space. The experience is compounded by colours of light that tinge the wall when the weather is clear. During morning services, the clerestory behind the congregation throws a delicate blue cast over the huge plane. At the same time, morning sun seeps through the wall from behind to tinge its cavities a pale lemon hue. The observer's eye intensifies these complementary colours by simultaneous and successive contrast, for as we stare at a blue or yellow area for a time, and then turn our eye to the other, that new colour is strengthened by an after-image of the same hue. Other, less salient shapes keep areas of wall from deadening, and help to unify the overall space. Among these accents are small punctures in the upper wall, their hidden sources reduced with height to emit a graduated sparkle. 'As the little windows get dimmer and dimmer,' Olli-Pekka Jokela remarks, 'they give a more dramatic feeling to the wall,' inflecting eyes to the rites below.

Detail of the altar wall

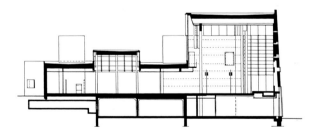

Above Altar wall with corner skylight beyond; *left* Section, looking north

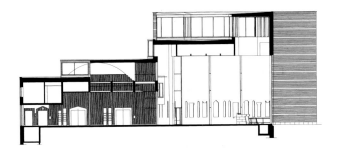

Above Interior with the altar at right; *top* Longitudinal section, looking south

ST MICHAEL CHURCH & PARISH CENTRE
HELSINKI, FINLAND, 1988
BY KÄPY AND SIMO PAAVILAINEN

The slight rotation of the two nested cubes that form this church also creates a residual zone where sunlight collects and softens before entering the room. As clerestory illumination fills the trough, it outlines and haloes the hall below; this ring of light is perceptually weighted to guide attention towards the altar. Narrow slits in the pink walls offer filamental views of nature, their cool tones cutting into and counterpointing the warm glow. The luminous envelope with glints of nature, and ceiling cut free by corrosive light, makes the church feel at once intimate and open, secure and adventurous. A different kind of radiant mass appears within the parish hall, where a glass shaft that contains the stairway fills to the brim with falling light, its silvery presence magnified by dim corridors – suggesting a transparent body where light has been trapped, like a pearl.

Above Staircase in the parish hall; *below* Plan

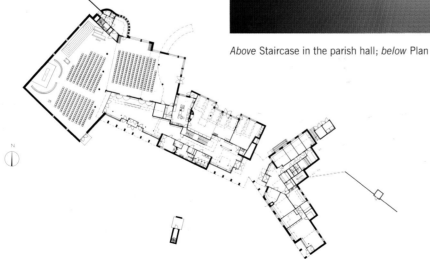

Ceiling and light troughs in the southwest corner of the church

Upward view of the vertical slits and light trough in the north wall of the church

Interior view, looking towards the altar

ST MAGNUS CHURCH
LILLESTRØM, NORWAY, 1988 BY LUND & SLAATTO

While owing a debt to the loosely jointed volumes of Dutch Structuralism and to Louis I. Kahn's Kimbell Art Museum in Fort Worth, Texas, the figure-ground reversal at Lund & Slaatto's St Magnus Church underplays its spatial components, and shifts attention to the light-slots between. No longer treated as merely a juncture for modular elements, the slot becomes the main protagonist as it invades solid form and carves the shell into fragments. Horizontal cuts through the vaults at their apex continue into vertical slits that extend to the ground. Additional slots cut away partial vaults and the higher vault over the altar, while other cuts dissect internal walls. Though some illumination reaches the ceiling, the vaults remain a half-lit backdrop for laser-like slits (unlike at Kahn's museum). The overall impression is of a room whose shell is repeatedly sliced by the power of light, both perceptually and spiritually, to the point of leaving materiality in shreds – giving light itself the power to trace new limits of space, and redefine architecture in metaphysical terms.

Continuation of the light slot in the interior walls

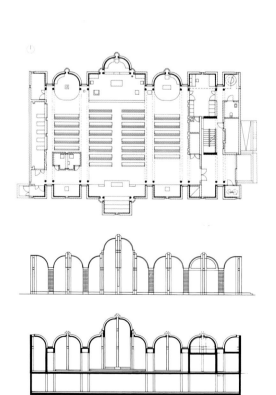

Above Westernmost vault of the nave; *left, above* Plan; *left, below* South elevation and longitudinal section, looking north

Serried light of the Finnish forest, Punkaharju

5

FOREST

The conversion of forest light into vessels and
frameworks of wood

Because Scandinavia remained in large part a rural society until well into the twentieth century, closely tied to the world of the forest, the region retains an intimacy with wood that continues to resonate in the Nordic soul.[46] The forest is where people lived and worked, and where they found the raw materials for their dwellings, furniture, boats and toys. Always more than a commodity, wood was considered a living material, permeated with myth and folklore, and treated in a manner that reveals and celebrates its innate structure.

Monolithic huts and cabins, still widespread across Norway and Finland, create an impression of being within the wood itself. The immersion is atmospheric, as well as material, for the continuous timber forms a vessel that collects and concentrates the aroma of wood, and presents a complex but unified whole, vibrant with light modulations, in which every tone contributes to the overall ambience. This consonance is immediately apparent in old peasant cottages that are built of nothing but logs and planks (see p. 122). Adding to the harmony are shadow-marks left by carpenters – cuts, joints, the bites of an axe and chips of an adze – and woodwork that has been worn smooth by touch or blackened by smoke. The ambience may not be bright, but it is nevertheless rich in mood, with a tawny glow that evokes the peace of the primeval forest. This atmospheric intensity is fully developed in Finland's eighteenth-century wooden churches. Illumination from low windows reflects off the unpainted and untreated pine

Brumunddal Church, Norway, 1965, by Molle and Per Cappelen

boards to fill the room with a dull glow, whose colour ranges from silky grey near the sun-washed floor to a warm golden hue in the faceted vaults and dome above. The result is entrancing, since all the objects coming into our field of vision are in some sense linked to the atmosphere that envelops them, and are consequently unified by a common spirit.

Even when reliant on industrial methods and standardized lumber, Scandinavia's recent timber architecture continues to draw upon primitive memories of the forest. Underlying this ethos is a belief that buildings should emanate from their genius loci, a notion captured in architect Reima Pietilä's off-quoted phrase: 'There are two kinds of

caves, caves of stone and caves of wood. The caves of wood are the dream of the people of the forest.' Among the many Norwegians who have tapped into these archaic feelings are Molle and Per Cappelen.[47] At their experimental timber house in Oslo (1962), the Cappelens tried to maximize the amount of untreated pine enclosing the space, and bathe this 'single, neutral material' with soft light from bevelled slots cut into the walls and vertical incisions at the corners. The same idea permeates their church at Brumunddal, Norway (1965; below), whose entire nave, from ceiling to fixtures, is built of pine. After filtering through a timber grill in the altar wall, and turning reddish-gold by repeated reflections, warm light spreads over the room to the point where it seems to condense and thicken, becoming palpable.

A more varied palette was employed by Sverre Fehn to echo the motifs of Norwegian painter Ingolf Holme for his studio–home in Holmsbu (1997; p. 122). The exterior is a remarkable fusion of boardmarked concrete and timber cladding, so closely matched in hue and texture that they blend into a monolithic mass, subtly striped with light and shade. The interior, by contrast, is a continuous sheathing that melds together different wood species and fabrications: an exposed frame of laminated beams, resting atop round steel columns; pine boards for floors and ceilings; and the slightly varying laminations of walls, doors and cabinets – giving free play to every sort of nuance and reflection within a totality of golden-brown light. A number of younger Nordic architects are also seeking to pare buildings down to vessels of wood, with an ambience that is archaic yet new. Carl-Viggo Hølmebakk's Sanderud Cottage (2004; p. 126), in Norway, deliberately tenses the primitivistic feelings of a hut with a cladding of machined plywood, together with soft, wooden recesses that face the vastness of the mountain scenery. The tapered and faintly organic wood cave of Matti Sanaksenaho's St Henry's Chapel (2005; p. 128), in Finland, draws upon equally poetic images that are simultaneously fresh and primeval, with its nearly animate void cloaked in shadows that slowly brighten towards the altar.

A complementary technique to satisfy Pietilä's 'dream of the forest' is cleft light, where illumination is broken up by a skeletal structure. The endless percolation of light in the forest has conditioned the way Scandinavians, the Norwegians and Finns in particular, see their world. Perhaps aeons of perception in a webbed landscape has led to a gradual adaptation to, and eventual preference for, the way things appear when veiled and filtered by fragments of light. The imprint of these patterns on the human imagination has been rewarded with an unsurpassed skill at using sticks to haze over space, carefully proportioning solid and void to tune the quality and degree of splintered light.

Alvar Aalto, an early virtuoso with screens, developed a repertoire of half-open baffles and grilles to finely modulate brightness and dimness, exposure and protection. His most eloquent expression of forest light is the Villa Mairea (1941; pp. 104, 132), where rustic poles and webbings of sticks minutely fracture the light passing through them, reminding us that the forest 'rustles' visually, as well as acoustically.[48] As recurring tones echo in place, a murmur is felt that is instantly calming. This soothing effect is based not upon mere repetition, as previously discussed, but upon tonal rhythms that shift and transform in beat and frequency. Unequal alternations of this kind also persist in Pietilä's architecture, where window frames have been deliberately proportioned to echo light patterns in the trees outside. Abstract and natural silhouettes are viewed simultaneously, arousing an active dialogue between inside and out.

Glacier Museum, Fjærland, Norway, 1991, by Sverre Fehn

In concentrating screens around the thresholds of doors, along with windows and balconies, Nordic architects are exploiting another dimension of fissured light, which reverberates in the human psyche at the deepest level. In the primeval forest, an ability to both see and hide – which largely determined survival – was maximized at woodland edges, where people could gaze out at the world from a place of retreat. This intermediate zone, at the border between the blur of the trees and the exposure of a forest clearing or open water, played a crucial role in our evolutionary development, as it did for many animal species. In its inte-

gration of what anthropologist Robert Ardrey called 'nest site and periphery', and geographer Jay Appleton terms 'refuge and prospect', the forest edge touches a nerve in everyone's distant memory. But the biological satisfactions of this primal space carry extra strength in the far North, where, until comparatively recently, the forest was everyone's home and haven against the outer world. Aalto's use of traceries around sensitive boundaries – from the pergolas of his Kauttua dwellings (1940) and the Kuusela housing block (1947) at the Sunila Pulp Mill, to his characteristic wrapping of stairs with clustered poles – arouse all these feelings; they protect the threshold with broken light, analogous to the outermost fringe of a forest lair. Other Nordic architects have continued to draw upon these images and traits from our evolutionary past: consider Gunnar Asplund's porticos, sheltering the chapels at the Woodland Cemetery (1940; p. 72), in Stockholm; Peter Celsing's latticework of wood through which visitors enter Härlanda Church (1959; p. 236) in Göteborg; the shifting density of wintry sticks around the foyers of Arto Sipinen's Tapiola Cultural Centre (1989; pp. 19, 123); or the detached webs that envelop Helin & Co's Finnforest Modular Office (2005; p. 125), in Espoo.

Among Norwegian architects, Sverre Fehn has been particularly drawn to the archetypal value of splintered light at domestic thresholds. The roots of this image are quite complex at his Schreiner House (1963), in Oslo. Surrounding the brick core and its clerestory light are timber caves that slowly dissolve into a loggia facing the garden – an homage to the northern forest, as well as to the skeletal edges of traditional Japanese houses and temples. The timber rooms are veiled behind a porous edge that is physically shallow but experientially thick, percolating forest light through three layers of posts and beams, mullions and slats, so as to gradually warm the fractured light and allow the dweller to gaze outside from a comforting thicket.

Although the Finnish sauna was originally an introverted space, tucked away in a dark earthen pit or log hut, growing stress is now being placed on its mediating function – as a graduated shelter into which people may slowly retreat for naked encounters with steam and darkness, but also from which they may cautiously emerge to plunge into a snowbank or forest lake. When gently blending inside and outside, the sauna embodies a primordial rhythm of ritual movement back and forth between refuge and outlook, heat and cold, darkness and light, fire and water. This dialectic is faintly evident in the portico and clustered poles of Aalto's sauna for Villa Mairea, and becomes the essence of Georg Grotenfelt's Huitukka Sauna (1982; p. 231), in Juva, Finland, a simple log hut covered with grass, which nestles in trees along the lakeshore and offers a balcony onto the world, while receding so completely into its site that we barely discern it from the landscape. Also based upon a mode of retreat that retains its horizon is Aarno Ruusuvuori's Bonsdorff

echoed the entry canopy with a timber trellis over the staircase. Illumination from a strip window filters through various layers of sticks, ranging from mullions and beams to borders of very thin slats, to give the impression of abstract tree-tops into which a person is climbing – an experience fulfilled in the pine-baffled windows and lofty trusses of the council chamber. In the student cafeteria at Jyväskylä University, this image extends over a wide space covered by openwork trusses, a structure conceived with far greater elegance in Kaija and Heikki Siréns' Student Chapel (1957; p. 136), at Otaniemi, Finland. The latter deserves special mention for the way its unforgettable light resonates with the surrounding forest. Below is a ground of plain red brick, its fired earth dark and compact; above is an airy canopy of pine, its branches suf-

Norwegian log house

Holme House, Holmsbu, Norway, 1997, by Sverre Fehn

Sauna (1985), which, set along the wooded bank of Lake Päijänne, transitions from an outer verandah through a dressing room and then washroom, to finally reach the sanctum of the sauna itself. The retreat inside to bathe and subsequent emergence are delayed and protected by successive layers of forest light, allowing even the innermost room a well-filtered view of lake and woods.

A slightly different experience is aroused by the sifting of light through a latticed ceiling, analogous to a forest canopy. A splendid example is Säynätsalo Town Hall (1952; p. 234), in Jyväskylä, Finland, where Aalto

fused in dappled light. Prayer occurs between the two, at the same time churchgoers gaze into the woods through a glass altar wall. Fehn employed a similar dialogue to return people to elemental conditions and deepen the human roots of his architecture. Hovering over the near-geologic foundations of his Villa Busk (1990), in Bamble, Norway, as well as the museums at Hamar (1979 and 2006; p. 86) and Fjærland (1991; p. 121), is a densely packed field of timber frames that unhurriedly filters natural light. As illumination trickles down, making some members glow and backlighting others, its flicker captivates the eye, while receding into space. The infinite lines, brushed with light, create an intimate forest inside the building envelope, with a poetic immensity that far exceeds its physical dimensions.

In their efforts to mine the psychological depths of porous woodwork and cleft light, a number of architects have been contributing new images to this taproot of Nordic culture. One such pioneer was the Helsinki firm of Kaira-Lahdelma-Mahlamäki (now Lahdelma & Mahlamäki), whose Forest Museum Lusto (1994; below) is visualized in cylindrical layers of toplit space and curved skins of wooden battens that line the concrete structure. From screens that guide visitors towards the entry to galleries wrapped with porous sticks, the infinitely fractured light of the forest is converted into geometric webs of larch, pine and alder.

The remarkable power to set us to daydreaming in several recently built churches in Helsinki, which are reduced to volumes of bare, softly glowing wood, is unavoidably linked to the simple austerity of old Finnish timber churches. But setting these churches apart, beyond their standardized lumber, is the prominent role of skeletal woodwork and the continual shredding of Nordic light, epitomized in the latticeworks and plaited skins of Järvinen & Nieminen's Laajasalo Church (2003; p. 140), which cause light to murmur wherever one looks. Based on similar sources, JKMM's Viikki Church (2005; pp. 144, 148) is even more emphatic in its reiteration of cleft light, and aimed to produce an 'all-wood atmosphere to evoke impressions of the Finnish forest, of its sacredness and common nature'.

Forest Museum Lusto, Punkaharju, Finland, 1994, by Kaira-Lahdelma-Mahlamäki

Tapiola Cultural Centre, Finland, 1989, by Arto Sipinen

This superabundance of metaphor reappears in two touching yet modest buildings by former partner Mikko Kaira, the daycare centres Misteli (1997) and Ruokopilli (1998), both in Vantaa, Finland. Inevitably recalling the refuge of a peasant hut, the former was built from massive logs that were treated with tar and linseed oil to emphasize the sensation of shelter, but also to yield a uniform texture that was sensitive to natural light. The serried image reaches a peak in the entry hall, where closely spaced wooden slats filter views and splinter sun, restoring an intimacy that is completely free of the picturesque.

The question of how far forest light can be abstracted, in order to loosen and deepen its capacity for interpretation, has been posed frequently by Aalto in forest-like screens made of non-wood materials, such as ceramic tile or copper, and by Henning Larsen in the brick elements that serve as sunscreens at Tuborg Nord (1999), in Copenhagen. In their search to explore these alchemic possibilities, Scandinavian architects are using industrial fabrication to redefine the psychic protection of forest light, while eliminating nostalgia for the past. A surprising poetic freedom is attained by avoiding direct associations with wood, thereby expanding the leeway for human imagination to participate in shaping its own experience. Sublimations of this kind underlie the strangely intimate feel of Finnish Constructivist architecture in the 1960s, its volumes defined by linear outlines and fuzzy edges without resort to visible woodwork. In the reduced matter of architect Erkki Kairamo's buildings, a network of rectilinear lines wraps the perimeter, with structural frames that feather into rails and poles, ladders and stairs. This poetic image, which continues to enchant and speak to us, dominates his semi-detached houses and apartment complexes from the 1980s and '90s, including the Hiiralankaari Apartment Block (1983; below, right), and at an urban scale the Itäkeskus Shopping Centre and Office Tower (1987). Rarefied down to outlines of light often traced by slender steel, the orthogonal

Rovaniemi Airport Terminal (1992; p. 81), also in Finland, the clean geometry is overlaid with differently scaled grids and gauzy sheets of steel mesh. These industrial membranes seduce the eye with blurry images and moiré effects that transform with a viewer's location. The flutter calls remotely to mind the needled depths of a conifer forest, but relates equally to the efforts of contemporary artists to activate perception by making the world slip in and out of focus, as found in the 'floating shadow planes' of American installation artist Robert Irwin, in which a series of elusive, semi-transparent scrims atomize walls, while keeping the eye of an observer entranced and perplexed.

At Heikkinen-Komonen's Finnish Embassy (1994), in Washington, DC, indistinct memories of the ancestral landscape derive largely from

McDonald's Office Building, Helsinki, Finland, 1997, by Heikkinen-Komonen

Hiiralankaari Apartment Block, Espoo, Finland, 1983, by Erkki Kairamo

webbings confer on buildings a barely sensed arboreal image, stirring an ancient satisfaction where one can see without being seen, and easily retreat to safety.

The minimalist and hard-edged steel buildings of Heikkinen-Komonen appear at first glance to epitomize post-rural life, and to be totally stripped of forest memories. But the tension between absolutely clear volumes and the shimmer of screens set before them – dissolving away surface and logic, while exciting the creative eye – seems uncannily familiar. At their McDonald's Office Building (1997; above) and

colours of light. Set on the crest of a wooded slope, the dark metal box is dappled with illumination from neighbouring trees, and the façade is similarly dotted with light from a bronze trellis and climbing vines. This naturalized illumination is further tinged as it interacts with closely matched building materials – refracting through green-tinted glass, and reflecting off the patina of copper panels and polished slabs of moss-green granite – weaving a Nordic spell that is closed to reason but felt by the heart at a single glance, touching off a subconscious reverie.

Finnforest Modular Office, Tapiola, Finland, 2005, by Helin & Co

Warm inner glow of wooden chambers

SANDERUD COTTAGE
ATNSJØ, NORWAY, 2004
BY CARL-VIGGO HØLMEBAKK

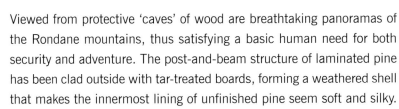

Viewed from protective 'caves' of wood are breathtaking panoramas of the Rondane mountains, thus satisfying a basic human need for both security and adventure. The post-and-beam structure of laminated pine has been clad outside with tar-treated boards, forming a weathered shell that makes the innermost lining of unfinished pine seem soft and silky.

The counterpoint of embrace and vista, the former seemingly shaped by rubbing and pressure from within, calls to mind another great image of contentment: Gaston Bachelard's nest-like house, as described in *The Poetics of Space*. Furthering this poetic experience is a monolithic treatment of pine, from smooth floorboards to the plywood skin of the walls and ceilings, not to mention the cabinets and drawers in which the objects of everyday life are hidden. It is not only Hølmebakk's use of a single material, but also that material's frequent folds and contrasting illumination that allow the warmly glowing wood to communicate a wealth of intimacy.

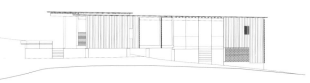

Above, left to right Children's bedroom; dining space; passage to the rear door; *top* Plan; *middle row, left to right* View of the corridor from the master bedroom to the living room; south elevation

Above, left to right Master bedroom; entrance and porch beyond; kitchen; view into house from the porch; *top* Detail of west elevation

Vestibule

Vestibule skylight and ceiling

Altar and side windows

Detail of south window and crucifix

Primal cave of wood

ST HENRY'S CHAPEL
TURKU, FINLAND, 2005
BY MATTI SANAKSENAHO

Conceived in plan as an abstract fish and in section as an overturned ship – two ancient symbols of Christianity – the chapel is nonetheless a new and unprecedented architectural experience. Melding the strangely tapered volume back into the forest is the green patina of its copper skin. The interior, by contrast, is totally finished with soft wood: pine for the laminated structural ribs, as well as for the untreated boards that line the walls and the waxed planks of the floor, all of which are closely matched to the benches of common alder. In addition to its aromatic and haptic appeal, the woodwork develops a mysterious atmosphere as small amounts of light play over its surface. Faint illumination enters the chapel at either end, only to die away in heavy shadows, at the same time highlighting ribs and tingeing the air a deep reddish-gold – dramatizing the long space as a spiritual quest. There is a slightly medieval character to the dusky path leading to light and the repeated glow of prayerful arches, but the wooden cave also exudes an animistic vitality that is closer in spirit to a modern wood sculpture by Henry Moore or Kain Tapper than it is to traditional church architecture.

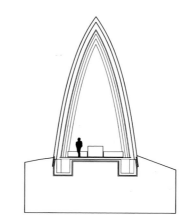

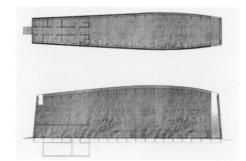

Above Overall view from the west; *top* Transverse section; *left* Conceptual plan and section; *below* Longitudinal section, looking north

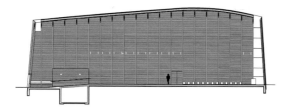

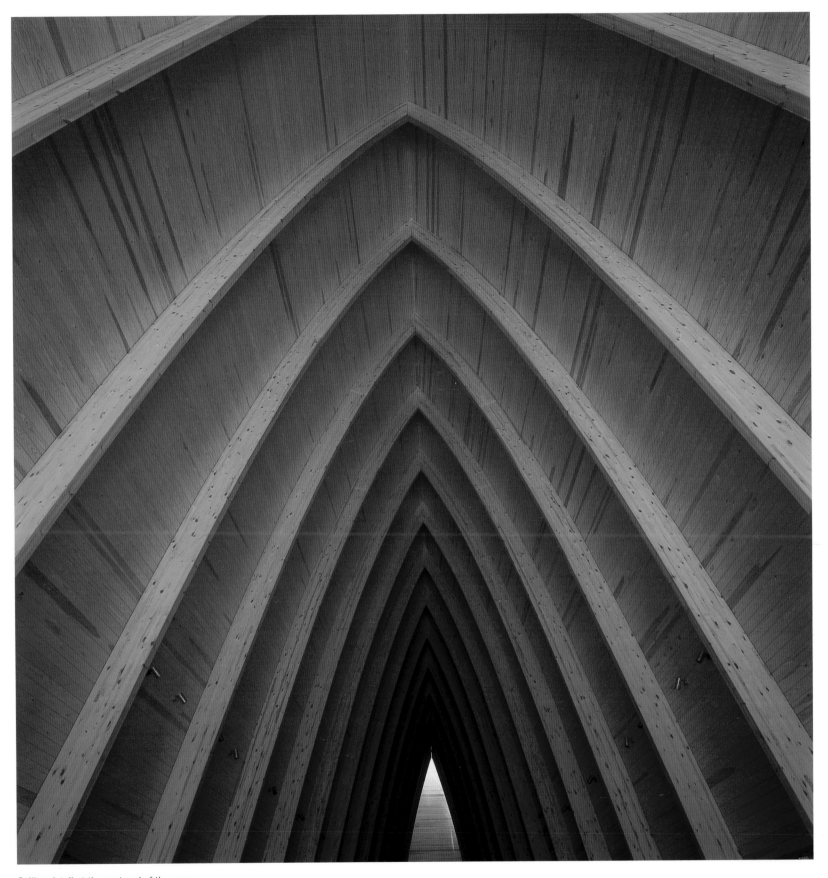

Ceiling detail at the east end of the nave

Upward view of the altar wall

Upward view of the vestibule from the passage into the church

Nave from the east

View back to the vestibule

VILLA MAIREA
NOORMARKKU, FINLAND, 1941
BY ALVAR AALTO

Every virtue of forest light has been poetically engraved in Aalto's Villa Mairea. The tonal play of sunlight across the timber cladding resonates with the bark, branches and leaves of the nearby woodland, while loose assemblies of post and beam, trellis and blind, and especially the rustic poles that have been lashed together with space between, evoke the serried light of trees. This experience returns at the living room steps, and then more densely around the stairway that leads to the bedrooms above. Here, the poles have been irregularly bunched and aligned into layers, parallel with the glass wall beyond, producing parallax effects for

the moving eye – the same relative motion experienced when walking through a stand of trees, as the farthest layer seems to move along with us while the nearest one slips away. A related image appears in the serpentine screen atop the library wall, which filters light from either side to create a stereoscopic impression that is reminiscent of backlit trees, particularly the broken light of a forest edge where rays diverge in criss-crossing streaks. Even the sheen of black steel columns contributes to a Nordic mood, making the rattan wrappings and surrounding woodwork appear to be fighting off an arctic chill with their warmth and relative brightness.

Above Sauna and pool; *below* Plan

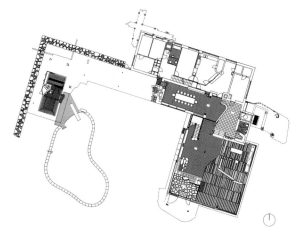

Above, left to right Main entrance; detail of door with its bronze, 'tree-branch' handle; detail of the sauna portico; entrance screen; *top* Overall view from the southeast

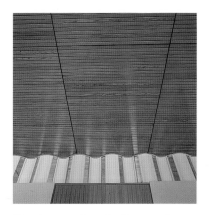

Glazed screen above the library wall

View to the living room from the winter garden

Passage to the fireplace corner, and the living room beyond

Main staircase with timber poles

Overall view from the south

Glass altar wall in summer, with a backdrop of forest and outdoor crucifix

Canopy of branching light

STUDENT CHAPEL
OTANIEMI, FINLAND, 1957
BY KAIJA AND HEIKKI SIRÉN

Hidden within a pine forest, the lacy screens of the courtyard and bell tower of this small chapel hint at the conversion of matter inside. Covering the building is a pine ceiling so beautifully crafted yet simply formed that it is almost unbelievable to behold. Untreated wood has been shorn of its bark, and milled to reveal the anatomy of its pale structure. Supporting the ceiling of natural pine boards is a complex trusswork, whose forking and branching lines are heightened by passing connections, as well as by the exposed bolts and black metal connectors. Light filters in from the clerestory to bathe over the skeletal woodwork, making it glow and appear to hover, as if percolating through a forest canopy, picking out vertical lines and tracing shadows along the way. Warmed in colour by each reflection, the illumination turns a deep gold before spilling onto the red-brick floor, restoring a lost intimacy with nature that repeats outside in the white cross, whose stark, austere form is dappled with shadows from the nearby trees.

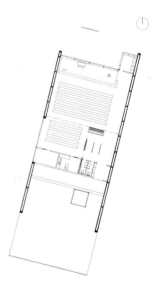

Above Detail of the courtyard fence; *top* Longitudinal section, looking west; *right* Plan

East wall with afternoon sun

Ceiling in the southeast corner

LAAJASALO CHURCH
HELSINKI, FINLAND, 2003
BY JÄRVINEN & NIEMINEN

Concealed within the shell of patinated copper is a world of nest-like spaces. Light enters the rooms by sifting through elegant layers of sticks, constructed at various sizes and scales to suit differing functions. The encounter begins in the entrance hall, with a trabeated structure clad with plywood of birch and pine, and is lined with delicate screens that mediate views and resonate with the trees outside. Doors with horizontal slits offer a veiled peek into the church. The sanctuary, conceived as a 'music box or wooden container', fulfills the promise of a spiritual retreat linked to the forest. Each part is constructed with lines of aromatic wood; even the solid planes are assembled from boards of contrasting grain to create a faint striation. A dense pergola covers the room, its doubled beams filtering light through wooden layers, suggestive of an overturned nest and emanating a feeling of security from above.

Above, left View from the northeast; *above, right* Longitudinal section, looking north; *top* North elevation; *right* Transverse section, looking west

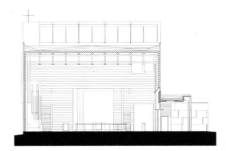

Above, left to right Altar wall at left, with side entry beyond; entrance hall, with side doors
to church at right; cloakroom; eastern edge of the church ceiling; *top* Entrance hall

Corner detail of the church

Detail of the sidelit timber relief in the altar recess

VIIKKI CHURCH
HELSINKI, FINLAND, 2005
BY JKMM

Externally coated with thick aspen shingles that have weathered over time, this sanctuary emits a flicker reminiscent of Finland's old wooden churches. These dotted vibrations transform into delicate screens lining the entry, whose finely knit grids are virtually translucent. The filtration shifts to serried light within the church, whose warm, hollow body is clad with multiple layers of lines that continually break the illumination into shards, which blur boundaries and half-dissolve walls. The lining of spruce is sensitized to light by a bleach of lye, making the finish unusually pale and luminous. One gazes not merely onto, but also into these walls, and, at one low window, out to nature through a porous filter of doubled posts. Here, light and view are further fractured by the spacings within and between members, complicating the layers of space that the eye may probe. Slivered light and plaited views culminate overhead in a dense truss of glulam beams. The interwoven sticks both branch out over and entangle space. As the lines of timber catch differing amounts and angles of illumination, and voids fill with uncertain shadows, an unlimited forest-like depth opens up for the mind to explore, while also evoking a heavenly canopy with distant architectural roots.

Above Overall interior view of the church, looking south; *top, left to right* Section looking east; section looking south

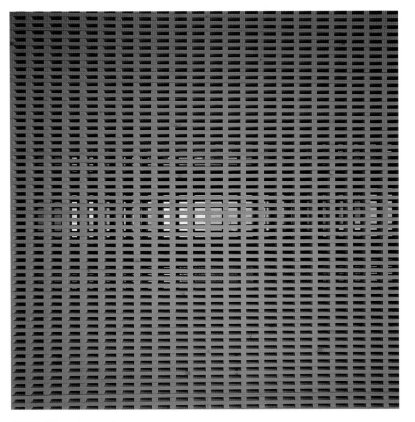

Detail of the entrance doors

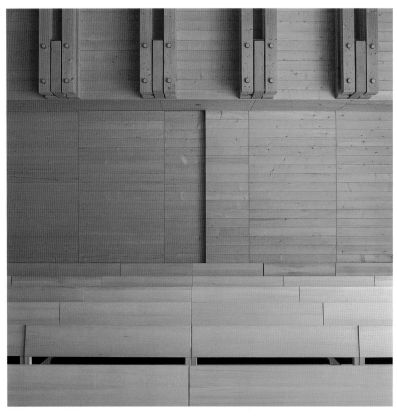

Detail of seating and east wall with sliding doors

Detail of the entrance hall

Church ceiling

Untitled, 2004–6, by Tor Arne

6

TRANSIENCY

The drama of expectation and loss in evanescent
displays of light

The subdued, dilute light of Scandinavia produces a haunting sense of transience, leading architect Kristian Gullichsen to observe: 'Up here in the North, in a way, we are waiting and waiting for the light to return.'[49] Even on midsummer days, when the sun circles the sky at low angles, there is a feeling of perpetual twilight. The further northwards one travels, the more the sky and land are bathed in a pensive atmosphere, until at the Arctic Circle there is nothing left but wistful, in-between tones. Throughout the region, winter days are shrouded in night, and summer nights are brightened by midnight sun. The impression of being caught in a fading moment brings a note of melancholy to Nordic light – a state of mind that artists and architects, along with poets and writers, film directors and composers, have sought to isolate and express. One

from the indistinct haze of summer evenings to lingering winter dusks, from early morning fog to the afterglow of sunset. Most beloved of all was midsummer night, when the world is suffused in a dreamy mist of blues, lilacs and bluish-greens, making it seem that the sky itself has descended to earth just as day has overtaken night. This half-light pervades the canvas in P. S. Krøyer's *Summer Evening on the South Beach at Skagen* (1893), portraying the molecular glow of a land caught between two seas and their vaporous weather. This unearthly haze is related to Scandinavia's 'blue hour', a condition enhanced by long dusks and the extreme refraction of the sun at high latitudes. Twilight continues to fascinate such contemporary painters as Finland's Tor Arne (see p. 146), who wrote: 'The light of those summer nights … I thought there

Århus University, Denmark, 1946, by Fisker, Møller & Stegmann

Viikki Church, Helsinki, Finland, 2005, by JKMM

thinks of the indefinable feeling of loss in Edvard Munch's violet-and-black series *Melankoli*, the drowsiness and expectant stillness in Vilhelm Hammershøi's pictures (see p. 8), the momentaristic space of Juha Leiviskä's buildings, the spare encounters with passing nature in poems by Bo Carpelan, the unfolding despair and bleak austerity in the films of Ingmar Bergman, and the ephemeral notes amid emptiness in the music of Estonian composer Arvo Pärt.

The plein-air painters of a century ago were especially drawn to the moods of twilight, and worked hard to capture their transitory states –

must be some way to capture this feeling in a painting. And sunrise, and the moment just before sunrise, the light coming into being. This is what joins us to all this, to all existence.'

Living within these ceaseless and bewitching mutations of light has sharpened the Nordic awareness of what the philosophers Henri Bergson and Susanne K. Langer termed 'duration' and 'lived time', respectively – the kind of subjective time that is known by the human body and soul, unlike the objective ticks of a clock.[50] Not since Britain's cosmic circles of megalithic stones, and the temples of Ancient Egypt, aligned to the rising or setting sun, has a building culture been so attuned to the moving sky, developing a virtually cinematic mastery over ephemeral light.[51]

Architects have invented a wide range of time-concepts to engage their buildings with Scandinavia's transient skies. Among the more modest techniques is construction based on a single material, whose uniform texture clearly exposes the shifting angles of moving sun. Finnish carpenters of the eighteenth century made full use of this effect, capping the rough log walls of their churches with intricate patterns of thick, wooden shingles. Alvar Aalto expanded this language with a variety of low reliefs based on monolithic skins. His corduroy surface of ceramic tile spreads a volatile shimmer over the Alvar Aalto Museum (1971; p. 79), in Finland, as light skims over ridges and shades valleys to completely

The sun's diurnal and seasonal cycles produce its most compelling drama, as the light of the world disappears and returns, dies and renews. By midwinter, the Nordic sun has largely vanished except for a brief appearance at noon, and even then remains low in the sky, seeming to neither rise nor set, but hover at the same spot in the south. As the only predictable access to sun throughout the year, this period and direction have provided a basic resource for architects searching to build an image of time true to its place, while maximizing the capture of daylight for practical reasons. The midday hour, as the sun reaches its zenith and crosses the meridian, has become both an architectural focus and a transformational event – providing yet another avenue to identify with life on the edge of the planet, and retain an intimate relationship with nature.

National Bank of Denmark, Copenhagen, Denmark, 1971, by Arne Jacobsen

Gug Church, Aalborg, Denmark, 1972, by Inger and Johannes Exner

alter the look of a wall. The architect was equally fond of bringing the stiffest matter to life under glancing sun, and instructed his masons to lay bricks at slightly different angles to one another. The resulting texture, especially at Säynätsalo Town Hall (1952; p. 234), also in Finland, appears flat under diffuse or frontal illumination, but vibrates as the sun arrives parallel to the surface. The mutability of rough brickwork was pushed even further in Denmark at places such as Århus University (1946; opposite), where Fisker, Møller & Stegmann covered simple volumes with a continuous crust of tactile yellow brick and tile.

The seminal work of regenerative light in Scandinavia is Erik Bryggman's Resurrection Chapel (1941; p. 79), in Finland, whose noon-time epiphany continues to influence the evolution of church architecture. Bryggman used light to portray a world in which life is not permanent, but fades and returns in ceaseless rhythms – a consoling image that helps people cope with the finality of death and experience it as part of a larger continuum, knowing that life will go on just as day reawakens after night and spring follows winter. This image of time has served as a model for architects of later generations, above all Juha

Leiviskä, who has in many ways surpassed his source in making daylong impressions of transient light the essence of architecture.

To understand evanescent light in the context of religious space, where most Nordic efforts have centred, its theological implications must be considered. The electrifying arrival of light within a church invokes, for believers, a divine appearance and transfiguration, as it has throughout the history of sacred architecture. In Scandinavian churches this 'coming of light' is generally produced by a hidden window, positioned south of the altar, which mysteriously spotlights the holy of holies and brings it into communication with the heavens. On each clear day of the year, the altar is briefly consecrated by light, giving visible form to the words in the Gospel of John that 'God is light' and that, as his son, Christ is 'the light of the world', able to overcome the darkness of the earth.[52] While divine light and visible light are not the same in Christianity, their correlation has been acknowledged since the Middle Ages, from the writings of Abbot Suger at Saint-Denis to the thirteenth-century treatise *De luce* by Robert Grosseteste. For two millennia of Christian thought and building, corporeal light has been considered a spiritual substance and,

above all things on earth, the most direct manifestation of God, the reality most similar to divine light, and the most seeable link between heaven and earth.

In addition to shaping their churches around this sanctifying force, Scandinavia's architects were also exploiting the everyday power of natural light to transcend earthly gloom, and, even more simply, to waken the world and bring it to life – a miracle inherently free of religious dogma and plainly evident to the senses. This entire spectrum is clearly at work in Leiviskä's churches, whose transformations peak around noon and exhibit a skill with mobile phenomena that rivals the art of film direction, a medium described by Russian film-maker Andrey Tarkovsky as 'sculpting in time'.[53] Before and after the climactic moments of midday sun are more leisurely flows of ambient colour, sent from the sky. These evolving hues give the North its world of moods, but are often so subtle and slow to change that the eye misses them. During overcast weather the atmosphere fades into chalky whites or greyish tones, while on clear days it chills into transparent blues. At dusk, the increasingly purple air is balanced by spots of radiant yellow as lyrical clusters of lamps come on, suspended in space. The colourful interplay touches a chord in the northern soul, with its starry image and vague recollection of peasant huts lit by fires, which for centuries held back the winter gloom.

Eclipsing the ambient tints at noon are brief but startling arrivals of sun, timed to coincide with religious ritual. 'In my churches', Leiviskä explains, 'the sun is to enter at the end of the morning service.'[54] It does not arrive all at once, however, but unfolds in a mounting progression, similar to the tensions and events of a musical score or film shot. The elements used to temporize light and give each church a unique orchestration are slots between parallel walls that are roughly aligned north to south.[55] The sun is thereby drawn into slits from one side at a preordained time of day. Blank white walls detonate in rapid sequence with dazzling streaks and patterns, their inclination tied to the season and turning reddish-orange in winter. At Leiviskä's Myyrmäki Church (1984; p. 22), in Finland, the sun appears gradually and crawls down a foreground plane, sliding over tactile wood slats to eventually brighten the entire wall facing the congregation, only to suddenly vanish before reappearing in a concentration

Opstandelses Church, Albertslund, Denmark, 1984, by Inger and Johannes Exner

Vardåsen Church, Asker, Norway, 2003, by Terje Grønmo

behind the altar. By contrast the altar walls at the Kirkkonummi Parish Centre (1984) and Männistö Church (1992; p. 154), also in Finland, ignite in a great crescendo and then die away, one by one, as various walls cut off the departing sun.

Leiviskä composed a fainter and more subdued effect for another Finnish church, the Church of the Good Shepherd (2002), at Pakila, which is based on layers of slender baffles that are no longer parallel but twisted to contrasting angles, and backlit rather than sidelit by sun. The ensemble slowly flickers to life as the baffles catch and bounce light from one to another, at times picking up colour from hidden paint. Counterpointing this flow are brighter notes with entirely different speeds, produced as the sun refracts through prismatic lenses between the hours of ten and twelve, casting arabesques and rainbow hues that rapidly alter with the advancing sun. The crescendos of Leiviskä's earlier churches are here replaced with delicate tremors, overlapping modes of time that come and go at varying rates, whose ethereal hues slowly converge behind the altar before disappearing. The common thread running through all of Leiviskä's churches is a daily reanimation of matter, as sunshine arouses the sleepy walls with a surge of energy and vital existence. The entrancing power of these displays stems in part from their breadth, which fills the visual field of the eye much like a theatre stage or cinema screen. These spectacles rival the most daring proposals for

light in motion envisioned during the 1930s by the Hungarian artist László Moholy-Nagy, whose 'light fresco' and 'fluctuating light-symphony' were intended to be painted onto the walls of a bare room, 'so that the white void should come to life and action under crossing sheaves of coloured light.'[56] The main distinction between Moholy-Nagy's and Leiviskä's ephemera is that the latter are slower and propelled by the cosmos, and thus continually point to a time and reality that lie beyond man – towards something infinite, and eternal.

Other Nordic architects are taking up the challenge posed by Bryggman and Leiviskä, shaping the arrival of light into a moment of sudden revelation when, in Mircea Eliade's words, 'something sacred shows itself to us'. Morning sun from a side window at Inger and Johannes Exner's Gug Church (1972; pp. 82, 149), in Denmark, for instance, brushes over an altar wall of rough concrete to suddenly make its quiet surface leap to life and palpitate, transforming the most humble matter into a wondrous apparition – an effect also achieved by Terje Grønmo with a ceiling slot at his Vardåsen Church (2003; above and p. 196), in Norway. Less restrained is the approach taken by Järvinen & Nieminen at their Laajasalo Church (2003; p. 140), in Finland, in their mutation of the altar recess at noon, where the sun grazes over a robust texture of cross-cut ends of wood to intensify its 'flickering pattern'. A related effort to exaggerate, rather than transfigure, matter occurs at

JKMM's Viikki Church (2005; pp. 144, 148), in Helsinki. In this case, the altar recess and bordering planes are silver-gilt to form a permanently luminous triptych, with the rear plane bent at its leading edge to expand the amount of trapped light and to create a double-phased solar arrival. While the material and somewhat decorative excess of the altar walls of the Laajasalo and Viikki churches undermine the purity of light, they also raise important questions about the limits of physical elaboration in creating a metaphysical event. Perhaps Arne Jacobsen anticipated the future of this balance at his National Bank of Denmark (1971; pp. 149, 184). Responding to the late-morning slices of sun are walls of sensuous marble plates, whose geologic texture and colour are sufficiently subdued, and devoid of aesthetic intent, to avoid diminishing the presence of light. At the same time, they are sufficiently uneven to throb into existence under glancing sun, allowing ethereality and materiality to coexist. As a result, the solar arrival in this huge empty space creates one of the most grounded yet awe-inspiring metamorphoses ever produced in secular architecture.

An attempt to not only transfigure the altar wall, but also to fold and stretch out the passage of time before and after, is seen in the modest Danish churches of Regnbuen Arkitekter, including those at Slagelse (2005; p. 36) and Silkeborg (2010; p. 40). Their white altar walls were shaped to be sequentially lit by glancing sunlight, accompanied by other events along the nave with contrasting speeds and dura-

Tapiola Church, Finland, 1965, by Aarno Ruusuvuori

tion. Illustrated here is a line of evolution, from the sunlit dramas of Erik Bryggman and Juha Leiviskä, which seeks to compound images of time by preceding or following the primary event with contrasting tempos and phrases of light.

Temporal complexities of this kind also play a central role in Simo and Käpy Paavilainens' churches, beginning with the twofold sequence of coloured light and beaming sun at Olari Church (1981; pp. 2, 218), in Espoo. 'Olari is timed for early morning,' explains Simo Paavilainen, 'between ten and eleven for the morning service. It was important that the light be impressive just then, allowing the sun to come in only at the altar, to concentrate everyone's interest. The sun reflects inside off a projecting brick wall, whose red-brick colour gives colour to the light and makes the altar space really red. This red colour is strongest before the service, when people are arriving. The colour is as important as direct sunshine, which comes to the altar around noon, making the altar seem distant from the rest of the church, and to feel like a holy space because it is strongly lit. After the service ends and the sun goes away, the light becomes dim and suddenly nothing is happening, and the show is over. It is suddenly quite quiet and a little dead, and you must wait until the next morning for life to begin again. It is a kind of miracle.'[57]

Transiency is further prolonged in the Paavilainens' Pirkkala Church (1994; p. 158), near Tampere, Finland, where splashes of sun on the altar wall transform in shape and position throughout the day. By liberating the image of time from any single slice of sky or privileged orientation, the Paavilainens instil their church with a continuously changing and less insistent religious dogma. This view is evidently shared by a number of architects, who are expanding the duration of mobile light beyond its role in a morning service. A simple example is Kaija and Heikki Siréns' Student Chapel (1957; p. 1362) at Otaniemi, Finland, where two prolonged phenomena – a diagonal shower of sun coming from behind, and a carousel of the seasons and weather beyond the glass altar wall – overlap in space and time. Some Finnish architects have gone so far as to de-emphasize the midday sun, including Lassila Hirvilammi, whose Klaukkala Church (2004), in Finland, features an altar wall that is streaked by sun in early morning and late afternoon, leaving the low south window behind the altar to dominate only in winter.

All pretence of a hieratic drama is abandoned in Aarno Ruusuvuori's concrete churches, where afternoon sunbeams shift spiritual emphasis away from the liturgical service and towards unprogrammed prayer. 'Light originates somewhere,' he says, 'but man does not need to know where. Lighting is not an end in itself. But its meaning is to create a feeling of the infiniteness of eternity.'[58] The dusky void of the architect's

Huutoniemi Church (1964; p. 242), in Vaasa, Finland, only comes awake under afternoon sun from a high corner window, its triangular beam gliding down the blackened wall to finally spotlight the altar. Apart from the occasional bar of sun cast by an overhead skylight, Ruusuvuori's Tapiola Church (1965; below and opposite, and pp. 8, 192) is also centred on the afternoon. During clear days (except in winter), a huge solar flash is directed onto the altar wall from the west, making a strong impression in the grey space. In spring and autumn, the incoming rays are patterned into a grid by the clerestory grill; in summer, the sun's higher altitude reduces penetration, but is augmented by additional beams through an angled slot above the grill, which boldly splash the altar. The result is that, roughly on the summer solstice, a mystical moment still celebrated through-out Scandinavia with bonfires and rituals, a trinity of light appears at the holiest spot in the church, but outside the range of liturgical authority.

One last image of time deserves mention: the building conceived as a ring of events that follow the circuit of the low Nordic sun, especially in summer during its travel around the horizon. This is the case at Vuoksenniska Church (1959; pp. 104, 160), in Imatra, Finland, where Alvar Aalto deployed light sources around the perimeter to identify and illu-minate different zones of the building, and set its collective space into motion with arriving and departing phenomena. Clearly his most metamorphic achievement, the church under-goes a clockwise progression of separate but varied illuminations. Other architects use quite different light-catching elements to produce an effect of circling time. The repertoire of horizontal and vertical slits deployed by Pekka Pitkänen at the Chapel of the Holy Cross (1967; p. 188), also in Finland, bathes different walls before and after the midday sun shoots down to the altar from paired rooftop channels. Slits are far more diverse and plentiful at Friis & Moltke's Hospital Chapel (2000; p. 164), in Denmark, where the climactic midday light of the chapel coexists with other incidents in subsidiary spaces, both indoors and out. All of these Scandinavian attempts to broaden the human experience of time find a

Tapiola Church, Finland, 1965, by Aarno Ruusuvuori

parallel in Le Corbusier's detonations at Ronchamp Chapel (1955) and the monastery at Sainte Marie de La Tourette (1960), both in France, through sources aimed to successive moments in the solar course.[59] But they also bear an uncanny resemblance to the *Skyspaces* of James Turrell, which celebrate celestial events from dawn to dusk and aim to give people a feeling of standing on the surface of the planet.

An alternate and more primordial way to gather the horizon, and form a larger world of space, is the building conceived as a perimeter of radial slits, an idea given magisterial power by Reima Pietilä at his Kaleva Church (1966; pp. 98, 170), in Tampere, and a more modest if equally touching expression by Inger and Johannes Exner at their Opstandelses Church (1984; pp. 16, 150), in Albertslund, Denmark. As in the circles of Stonehenge and the medicine wheels of the Native Americans, these two Nordic churches share an attempt to communicate in a revolving manner with the sky. As periodic sunbeams enter the former from constantly shifting directions, their coming and going is heralded on shuttered concrete. By contrast, each of the latter's angled planes is bent at the end to overlap its neighbour, forming between them hidden slits that the sun can slip through in turn and arouse its wall of uneven brickwork. The chronology and space of these radial churches may be less precise than that of the ancients, but they are now enhanced by the continuous mutation of a habitable space. The churchgoer knows, in the same precognitive and Ptolemaic way as in the past, that he or she stands in a place anchored into the universe, just as that universe has entered inside to shape a reality that is far more real than the physical building.

MÄNNISTÖ CHURCH
KUOPIO, FINLAND, 1992
BY JUHA LEIVISKÄ

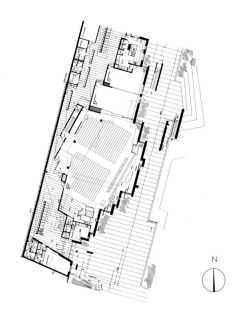

The consciousness of time at Juha Leiviskä's Männistö Church develops around its multilayered altar walls. Initial signs of change are subtle, as ethereal tints of coloured light, which reflect from hidden patches of paint on the rear of walls, appear without any visible source and intensify with the advancing sun. From out of an overall misty whiteness, these pale hues deepen before reaching a peak, to be suddenly displaced after noon by sunbeams shooting inside. As direct sun arrives tangent to the altar walls, it illuminates each plane in rapid sequence from far to near. The grainy plaster casts its own miniature shadows, with bluish tones that complement the warm sunshine, to produce a faint pointillist interplay until the sun arrives more obliquely to bleach the surface to dazzling white. Like morning fog burning off, the church's soft colorations are displaced by a radiance that is clear and hard, its beams sharply etched by the shadows from mullions. Though walls are parallel and belong to the same slice of sky, the architect has modified the 'pitch' and 'duration' of each slot by varying its depth and external projection. It is the arrangement of these slight variants, much like the strings of a musical instrument, which orchestrates the temporal phrases and makes a lyrical whole of the solar display. As walls gradually shade one another, the brilliant array fades and shrinks in a complicated diminuendo, to finally leave the wall immediately behind the altar illuminated, as if by a spotlight before the final curtain comes down.

Above Overall view from the south; *top* Ground-level plan of church

Above Altar engulfed in sunlight; *top, left to right* Altar wall: morning; midday; soon after midday; early afternoon

Final note of sun behind the altar

Layered washes of sun on the altar wall

PIRKKALA CHURCH
TAMPERE, FINLAND, 1994
BY KÄPY AND SIMO PAAVILAINEN

The most remarkable aspect of the suspension of ordinary time at Pirkkala is the complexity with which its tempos develop, breaking or merging into temporal phrases that keep transforming throughout the day. The slowest mutations occur outside on the white brick walls, which vividly show the evolving spectrum of sun and sky. More startling effects are produced inside on the curved altar wall, made responsive to shifting light by layered paints, in which a translucent white wash is brushed incompletely over a lustrous white ground. Direct sunlight arrives on this wall, especially in summer, from a wide range of angles, controlled by a continuous slot that begins as a twisting clerestory and ends in a vertical window to the west. The consequence of this manifold source is that beams of sunlight are spattered without interruption on a single projection screen, from late morning to sundown, and these projections mutate continuously in number and size, location and shape. At times, light is thrown onto different areas of wall, or overlaps in a collage when the glass behaves as both lens and mirror. As the pale-blue cast of morning clears, sunshine arrives in a series of arcs that gradually rise and coalesce in a wavy band, to culminate in a growing mass of western sun that acts out the final drama.

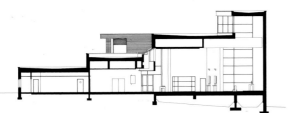

Above Altar at midday; *top* Transverse section looking west

 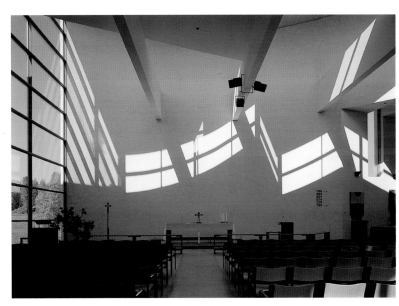

Light sequence on altar wall: *top row, left to right* Early morning; late morning; *middle row, left to right* Midday; early afternoon; *bottom row, left to right* Mid-afternoon; late afternoon

VUOKSENNISKA CHURCH
IMATRA, FINLAND, 1959
BY ALVAR AALTO

The remarkable sequence on long, summer days begins in the morning as the eastern sun slips inside through twin slits at the side of the altar. Baffled by fins, these openings cast parallel beams without any visible source. Nearby and active throughout the morning are three 'crystal windows' in the east wall, whose differently angled sheets of glass bounce the arriving rays back and forth to make the cavities sparkle and glow. Just as the morning service concludes, sunlight enters once again, but more mysteriously, as beams shoot down from a rooftop tube aligned with the southern sky. While guiding soft skylight onto the altar for much of the day, these tubes are angled to briefly catch the summer sun near its zenith. For a matter of minutes, the brilliant stream spotlights the altar, while bouncing off the white marble floor to cast strange, overlapping tones on the crosses behind – concluding the ceremony with a touch of magic. Also around noon, at the rear of the church, sunlight appears in a series of skylights above the south doors, dividing morning from afternoon and setting the stage for a new progression around the west side of the nave. As the westerly windows come into play, some slatted and others tubular, the church undergoes a sequential animation from south to north. Finally, as the sun sinks lower in the sky, it fills the church with a bewitching ambience. Golden rays slanting in from the west are further warmed by reflections off the pine pews and floorboards, to completely paint over the snow-white plaster and make reality fall away in a delirious veil of colour.

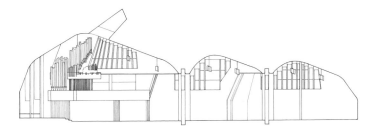

Above Detail of the east elevation; *top* Longitudinal section, looking east

Entrance hall

Ceiling with warm, reflected light in late afternoon

Interior looking south in the afternoon

Above, left to right View towards the altar in mid-afternoon; east side of the nave in mid-afternoon; *top* Altar struck with midday sun from the rooftop channel

   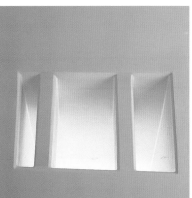

Above, left to right East windows of the nave; morning sun on three crosses; reflections and shadows from the midday sun; rooftop channel in late afternoon; *top* Altar wall, with twin beams of morning sun

Water court, looking west

Northeast corner of the water court

Seating alcove, north corner of the water court

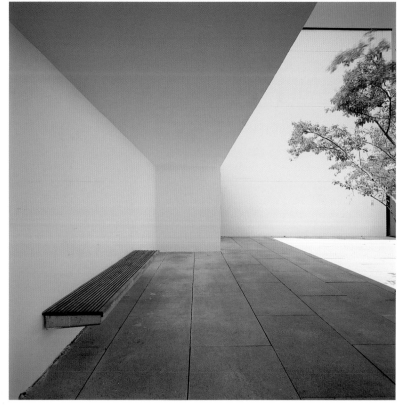

Seating alcove, south wall of the water court

Manifold slits and washes of sun

HOSPITAL CHAPEL
AALBORG, DENMARK, 2000
BY FRIIS & MOLTKE

A composition of nested walls, built out of white concrete, allows the sky to paint neighbouring zones with contrasting moods – a coexistence of temporal states that begins outdoors in the entry court and concludes in the chapel. Paralleling these slow mutations are rapidly moving slices of sunlight, which progress through a wide assortment of slits cut into the seams of intersecting planes. The most transformational of these are positioned at ritual junctures: window strips bordering thresholds; a glazed void open to sky at the turn into the chapel; and roof slits at either end of the chapel itself. The latter's resurrective message appears around noon, as first one, and then the other wall is washed by a sheet of moving sunlight, which flows initially down the rear plane to skim and animate its tactile surface, before reappearing at the eastern end to flow up the altar wall. To one side of this dual event is a more prolonged temporal structure – a skylit slot just beyond the glazed south wall, whose continuous solar cycle is tied conceptually to its Möbius sculpture. Providing yet another mode of time are unstable reflections on the metal cladding of doors and cabinets, a dark coppery-red tombac whose blurry and patinated sheen can suddenly flare up with reflected light and just as suddenly die away.

Above Overall view from the south; *below* Longitudinal section, looking south

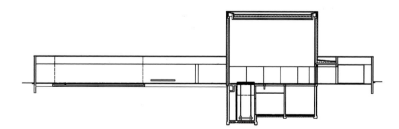

Entrance

Chapel door

Above Arrival sequence of midday sun on the rear wall of the chapel; *top* The chapel in late afternoon, with the outdoor light slot beyond

Above, left to right Passage to the mortuary; view to the entrance hall from the chapel; the main doors from the entrance hall; the glazed court from the chapel door; *top* The glass-enclosed court, near the chapel doors

Image of radial time

KALEVA CHURCH
TAMPERE, FINLAND, 1966
BY REIMA PIETILÄ

Scandinavia's most powerful image of radial time, Reima Pietilä's Kaleva Church, is essentially an irregular ring of towering pillars, divided by slits – a solid–void alternation that resembles, both physically and cosmically, a prehistoric ring of stones. Each slit frames a different slice of sky, receiving sunlight at a unique and particular hour of the day, according to the season. Before and after shooting inside from each slot in turn, the sun skims over deep reveals of battered concrete to make the enclosure pulse with existence. Every flash across the nave appears for a time, and then fades away as the next window comes into play and sends inside a fresh beam at a new angle. The vast height of the space and its hilltop site allow the sun, even at its summer zenith, to rake over the pews and penetrate deeply into the church. The winter sun, by contrast, is almost horizontal and leaps over the nave to splash its far walls. When sitting in the church for any length of time, it is possible to follow a clockwise progression as the shafts of light come and go, slanting in from a circle of points to mark out time like a huge sundial.

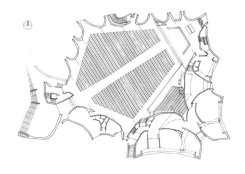

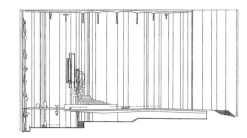

Above Overall view from the west; *top* Sketches of light and shadow within slits and plan; *above, right* Plan; *right* Longitudinal section, looking south

Above, left to right The interior: without sun; with early afternoon sun; with late-afternoon sun; view across pews to the choir;
top Afternoon view towards the altar and its backlit sculpture, *The Broken Reed*

Sunlight fading from slot at left and appearing in slot at right

Upward view of light slot between concrete piers

Neighbouring light slots with different sections of sky

Afternoon sun on neighbouring piers

Play of diffuse light over the faceted concrete

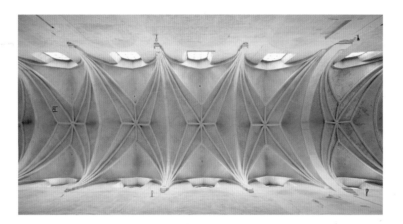

Turku Cathedral, Finland, 14th century

7

TRANQUILLITY

The peaceful glow and solitude of unadorned things
reduced to their essence

Lying at the heart of Scandinavian architecture is an air of tranquillity. Bare materials and direct techniques, enhanced by the stripping away of inessential gestures and decoration, immediately calm building forms, while endowing them with a quiet dignity. This sense of restraint stems in part from peasant life, when the availability of few materials in a severe climate encouraged the most frugal construction, the roots of which are renewed every summer in retreats to deliberately rustic cabins. But it derives also from geographic seclusion on the outskirts of Europe, where it is necessary to come to terms with the solitude of an arctic climate and its bleak moods.

Over time, these constraints evolved into a cultural ethos that now seeks beauty in unadorned things, reduced to their essence. Among the

fabric of pale bricks has a bleaching effect on the interior space, yet compensates for this colour reduction with a mellow, spiritual light. Appearing on the chalky vaults are imperceptibly frail highlights and transparent shadows that accentuate one another as they interact on spare details. All of these greyish-white tones contribute to a unified mood, producing an atmosphere of silence that is instantly felt long before it is consciously noticed.[60] The same preference for tonalism and monochromatic harmonies can be followed in Scandinavian painting, suggesting a sensibility that is drawn more to nuanced light than to conspicuous form – a stress wonderfully captured in Vilhelm Hammershøi's *Interior* of 1901.

In addition to wood, another material that is widely employed in Nordic lands to bring a self-assured modesty to buildings is brick, used

Tampere Cathedral, Finland, 1907, by Lars Sonck

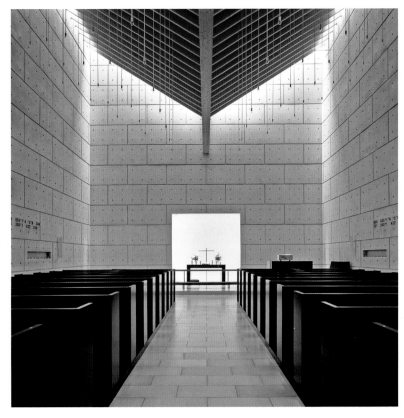

Enghøj Church, Randers, Denmark, 1994, by Henning Larsen

benefits of this search for the elemental – from the gently ascetic buildings of Alvar Aalto and Arne Jacobsen, to the trabeated extrusions of Sverre Fehn and the tough, industrial boxes of Heikkinen-Komonen – is a stark revelation of Nordic light. Even medieval cathedrals, such as that at Turku, in Finland (p. 174) were pared down to a state of grace, moving away from exuberance, rhetoric and iconography in favour of an understated plainness that would have seemed out of place in central or southern Europe. A similar worship of simple refinement is evident in the thirteenth-century Västerås Cathedral, in Sweden, where the continuous

to create bare, tactile walls that stand on their own, free of adornment. Especially responsive to faint light is the pale yellow brickwork of Denmark, seen to best effect in the superbly austere Grundtvigs Church (1940; p. 180) by Peder Vilhelm Jensen-Klint and the intensely plain cubes of Fisker, Møller & Stegmann's Århus University (1946; p. 148), whose every component, from pavement to column, was built from the same substance. Enhancing the soft chiaroscuro is a suppression of all extraneous details that might disturb the peaceful unity and unbroken passage from plane to plane, so that every facet offers a slightly new modulation of one overall ambience. Other Danish architects have been drawn to this reticent palette, including Inger and Johannes Exner at their Sankt Clemens Church (1963; p. 75) and Jørn Utzon at his housing complexes at Helsingør (1959) and Fredensborg (1965). In producing different shades of the same quiet hue, these buildings convey a great truth: that any truly compelling atmosphere is based on a serenity that avoids monotony, whose tones force us to look at them again and again.

Barren stone offers yet another resource for creating a solitude suited to the North. Among Lars Sonck's many remarkable feats at Tampere Cathedral (1907; opposite) is his chiselling of shadows into continuous granite to quell the figuration of massive walls, and thereby temper the decorative, nationalistic zeal of Finnish Romanticism. Arne Jacobsen, by

cushioned effects are complemented inside by an attenuation of linear matter, with columns and beams, mullions and rails, treads and benches, pared down to almost nothing. Having all but their final essence removed, the skeletal forms conjure up a mute and spiritual kind of poverty, standing against a glowing emptiness, brought to the boundary between being and nothingness. Consisting mostly of thin air and disembodied lines relieved of matter, the ghostly objects are rendered transparent and absorbed by light, a metaphysical shift that also underlies the Finnish buildings of Kirmo Mikkola and Erkki Kairamo.

Undoubtedly the most humble material used to 'construct' silence in Nordic architecture is raw concrete, with all its coarseness and burrs intact. It is a substance ideally suited to churches, where solemnity and

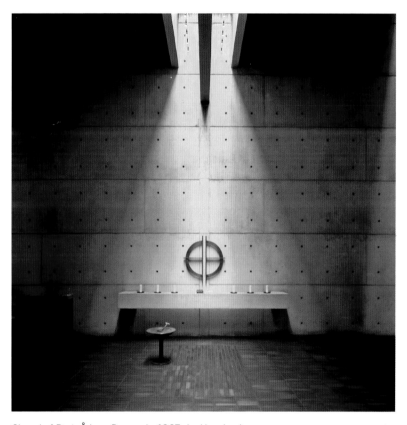

Resurrection Chapel, Woodland Cemetery, Sweden, 1925, by Sigurd Lewerentz

Chapel of Rest, Århus, Denmark, 1967, by Henning Larsen

contrast, handled stone in a painterly, rather than sculptural, manner, in order to ease and massage his boxy masses. The almost alchemic transmutation of hard marble into something that appears airily soft occurs in the cladding of his town halls at Århus (1942; pp. 7, 52) and Søllerød (1942), and later the National Bank of Denmark (1971; pp. 149, 184). Grey veining produces a quietly tense skin, which is gently aroused at every point by tonal vibrations that drift over one another and dissolve away surface planes. Strengthening the misty impression are simply detailed windows and an unbroken flow of stone around corners. These

poverty have religious connotations. Among Finland's early exponents of concrete as spiritualized matter were Keijo Petäjä, with his Lauttasaari Church (1958), and Pekka Pitkänen at his Chapel of the Holy Cross (1967; p. 188), who used a gentle stillness to soothe and comfort an overwhelmingly vacant space, thus offering sanctuary of a special kind. The same minimalist spirit is apparent in Aarno Ruusuvuori's concrete churches of the 1960s, including those at Hyvinkää (1961; p. 60), Huutoniemi (1964; p. 242) and Tapiola (1965; pp. 8, 152, 153, 192), all of which were kept totally bare apart from the play of light and shade on structural details. The emptiness of all these churches is made poignant by the leaving of so much of their walls blank, in the same way that most of the surface of a Japanese ink-wash painting is left untouched, to make the void itself palpable and become the main subject of the picture.

At Viljo Revell's Vatiala Cemetery Chapel (1960; p. 230), in Finland, space has been calmed to a state of numbness. The heavy shadows gathering in the parabolic vault absorb the few rays of dying light that are allowed to enter. Adding to the silence are plain walls of fair-face concrete and brownish grey sound-absorbent panels that line the vault, complemented by dark-stained timber pews and floors of foundry-cast concrete slabs, touched here and there with dark bronze fittings, weaving an atmosphere from which all living colour is leached. The smoky light that falls on such muted forms feels peaceful yet sombre, and strangely remote, all but eluding our senses. Soft greys shift awareness to the elusive air between solid things, and away from the things themselves – a detachment from reality that is heightened by glass walls that open onto placid sheets of water. As every surface is anaesthetized and fades away, left behind is a melancholy state where death pervades life, not as a menace but as an inescapable shadow.

Underlying the sobriety of Finland's concrete churches is an 'active aesthetical appreciation of poverty', which closely parallels the Japanese principles of *wabi* and *sabi*, described by philosopher Daisetz Suzuki as the essence of Zen and epitomized in lonely mountain temples.[61] Pared down to barren grey shells, neither Japanese temples nor Finnish churches are left fully vacant, however, for they fill by day with a pensive mood that endures and commands respect. Stripped of every other distraction, light and shade become the sole 'decoration' of rooms that would otherwise revert to mere voids. Danish architect Henning Larsen has pointed to another way of emotionally charging raw concrete, by painting its surface with visiting hues of natural light – an art indebted to Louis I. Kahn and, more recently, Tadao Ando. Ethereal tints in a grey void largely define Larsen's Chapel of Rest (1967;

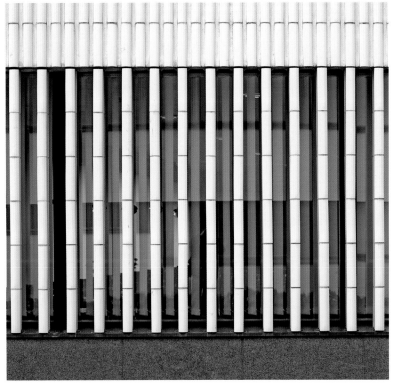

Seinäjoki Theatre, Finland, 1987, by Alvar Aalto

p. 177) in Århus, Denmark, where a warm prism of diffuse sun falls like a spotlight onto the altar and the remains of the dead. Cooler tones prevail at the Enghøj Church (1994; p. 176), also in Denmark, as skylight washes down over the walls and seeps through from behind to make the bluish-grey cast sparkle. Enriching the atmosphere are warm reflections from the timber ceiling, and contrasting greys from the bright altar recess to the polished stone floor and lustrous black pews. The result is a meld of silver grey, violet grey, brown grey, dove grey and, at times, plain grey – that colour devoid of all colour. Similar intonations shape the gently forsaken mood of Terje Grønmo's Vardåsen Church (2003; p. 196), Norway, and the spiritual serenity of the architect-monk Hans van der Laan's Benedictine Abbey (1995; p. 198), in Sweden, the latter a providential match between soft Nordic light and the contemplative aims of its creator.

Two kinds of solitude coalesce in Sigurd Lewerentz's Resurrection Chapel (1925; p. 177), whose exhausted light brings a Nordic moodiness to the classical language of the south. The melancholy originates in the restrictive palette of ashen materials: window and door frames of white marble, and plastered walls that have been painted over with wax-based pigments, conveying age and weathering, set off by a pebbly floor of grey marble mosaic. The interior is not merely colourless but astringent, even deathly. Illumination aimed to the catafalque from a single window intensifies the lament for the dead, while casting odd upward shadows and a thin, overall chiaroscuro. Everything is mute and still in this empty room, where the poverty of light expresses the chapel's elegiac function, endowing the space with an aura of desertedness that is dismal yet curiously poetic.

A very different lesson in solitude is drawn from buildings that are gently detached from their surroundings by an intervening atmosphere – withdrawn behind a fogginess that calms the objects it veils. Amorphous outlines of this kind are a common sight in the North, since the air through which the world is viewed is often moist. Scandinavian painters have long been captivated by translucid air, from Hammershøi's silver-grey spaces to the final canvases of Finnish artist Pekka Halonen, their whitish-grey winter tones thinned down to transparent washes. Abstract artists, too, continue to pull cognitive reality out of focus and bring a more active dream-like reality to the surface of awareness, as seen, for instance, in the paintings of Tor Arne (see p. 146), which convey a world fully absorbed into the coloured air, presenting nothing but vague shapes of molecular light.

One method of fogging the solid form of a building is to clothe its façades in a hazy medium. This elusive image is readily apparent in Alvar Aalto's claddings of semi-cylindrical white tiles, which pass over windows, cloaking the mass with a film that vibrates in front of its surface. Fascinatingly inaccessible and ephemeral scrims are being invented in a wide variety of materials and forms, often doubling as sunscreens while blurring views and enveloping space in a quiet reticence. The result turns desolate at Larsen's Mærsk McKinney Møller Institute (1999; p. 75), at Odense University, where darkly screened windows are isolated in foggy grey walls. At JKMM's Turku City Library (2007; right), the exterior render is coloured to suggest molecular dissolution and textured to match the equally mottled glass louvres that protect the windows – making the façade indefinable, as if wrapped in mist. A comparable effect appears in Lahdelma & Mahlamäki's Iiris Office Building and Service Centre for the Visually Impaired (2004), in Helsinki, where translucency blurs every window and increases

Turku City Library, Finland, 2007, by JKMM

with height to culminate in a nebulous volume atop the building – a solitude lost in the clouds.

A quite different technique to defocus form is the casting of ultra-soft highlights and shadows onto a bare volume from many directions. As the fluid tones meld while washing over walls, their amorphous shapes stand in space while obscuring the physical contours behind. Aalto often achieves this state with long, trailing shadows from multiple skylights, causing the tones to intermingle and cling to the surface like suspended layers of fog or smoke. Rather than being an end in itself, the boundary serves as a projection screen for the elusive tonalities that are brushed

on its surface. Vague penumbras that elude definition are a predominant presence in Aalto's church at Riola di Vergato (1978; p. 16), in Italy, where light is sprayed onto vaults from three scalloped monitors, casting an array of imprecise tones that seem airbrushed on, veiling the church in a dreaminess that is free, in part, of any solid object.

An alternate means of blurring architecture is to delaminate walls and dissolve their layers into the light filtered through them. This phenomenon appears in Aalto's staggered baffles, but reaches its apogee in the churches of Juha Leiviskä, where we encounter a solitude that is truly mystical. Boundaries have been broken down into parallel planes that overlap, so that layers emerge from behind one another in a series of protruding edges. Receding space melts away in the intervening atmosphere and shifting focus of a human eye. Everything takes on an airy, vibrating look, precisely the effect of aerial perspective common to the vaporous North.

Physical elements and material dissolution, however, are ultimately less important to Leiviskä than the way glancing light is induced to linger on baffles. Each plane appears as a backdrop behind its own thin layer of light, which in turn seems trapped between the planes, leaving an elusive glow as the only real presence. The ebb and flow of residual light produces the kind of levitation that Kazimir Malevich envisioned in his 'absolute paintings', aimed to 'express the sensation of flight ... the feeling of wireless telegraphy', where 'white on white expresses the feeling of fading away ... a magnetic attraction', as in a 'wave' from 'outer space'.[62] Equally crucial to Leiviskä's effort to isolate space in a mystical fog is the layering of varied intensities of light, producing tones that advance or recede independently of the planes they are viewed against, but not derived from. Nothing is left to distract from the numbing display of an insubstantial atmosphere, seeping in as if by spiritual osmosis. At the brink of nothingness, and deprived of outward expression, the walls exert an introspective glow and draw us into an arctic solitude.

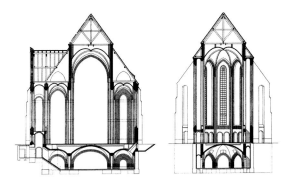

Golden air of yellow brickwork

GRUNDTVIGS CHURCH
COPENHAGEN, DENMARK, 1940
BY PEDER VILHELM JENSEN-KLINT

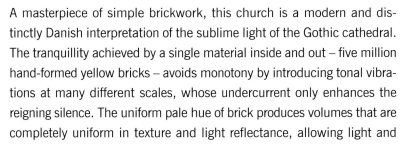

A masterpiece of simple brickwork, this church is a modern and distinctly Danish interpretation of the sublime light of the Gothic cathedral. The tranquillity achieved by a single material inside and out – five million hand-formed yellow bricks – avoids monotony by introducing tonal vibrations at many different scales, whose undercurrent only enhances the reigning silence. The uniform pale hue of brick produces volumes that are completely uniform in texture and light reflectance, allowing light and shade to define forms according to how each new facet is orientated with respect to windows. The clarity and strength of form achieved by a monolithic volume is especially impressive inside the building, where a rich, golden atmosphere develops from seemingly infinite modulations of one space-enclosing substance. With all decorative elements removed, including overtly religious iconography, a deep sense of peace is established, where all attention is thrown onto the utterly quiet and soaring lines of ethereal light.

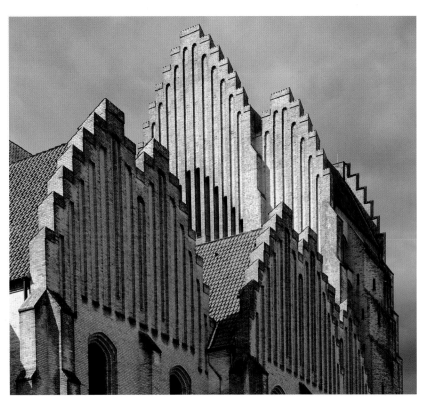

Above Detail of the gable roofs; *top* Transverse sections; *below* Plan

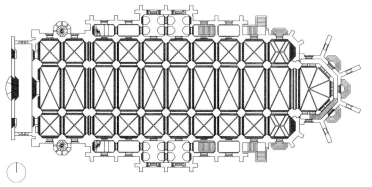

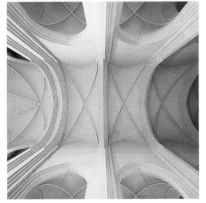

Above, left to right Upward view of the nave vaulting; aisle vaulting and edge of the south gallery; nave vaulting; aisle piers; *top* South aisle and pulpit

View of nave from the west

North aisle from the west

South aisle from the west

Windows in south transept

Blind arches and staggered piers

Above, left to right Chiaroscuro at west end of the entrance hall; entrance and glass passage; entrance hall without sun; entrance hall with late-morning sun; *top* Glancing sun on the marble plates of the east wall

Barren space taken over by blurry shadows and slender sunbeams

NATIONAL BANK OF DENMARK
COPENHAGEN, DENMARK, 1971
BY ARNE JACOBSEN

Following an exterior that seems cloaked in mist, and an eerie descent through a tube of glass, the bank's entry hall is haunting in its feeling of absence and withdrawal from the city. The cathedral-like volume, lined with grey marble, is excruciatingly bare, apart from a few small pieces of furniture. The attenuated lines of one lonely but dramatic staircase, suspended from the ceiling, amplify the vacancy while adding a hint of levitation and magical ascent. Pressing into this picture of solitude are emanations from double slits in the south wall, which cast blurry shadows and brief sunbeams into the solemn yet elegant space. Because everything else has been taken away, the invading tones are greatly exaggerated in importance, to the point of becoming the only real presence and completely taking over the void.

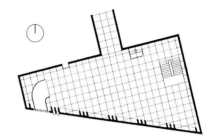

Above Southeast corner of entrance hall; *top* Plan of entrance hall

Upward view of the entrance hall ceiling

Entrance hall from the west

Bottom of the staircase

Suspended staircase

Curved glass entrance passage

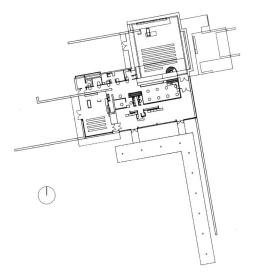

Hypnotic stillness of bare concrete and solitary pools of light

CHAPEL OF THE HOLY CROSS
TURKU, FINLAND, 1967
BY PEKKA PITKÄNEN

This chapel's pale and desolate volumes – from the exterior masses, secluded in pine trees, to the ascetic voids within – create a feeling of isolation far removed from the outer world. Barren walls of poured concrete are left untreated, and are supplemented by a smooth finish of prefabricated concrete slabs, their grey scale relieved by only a few sparse details of bronze and oak. Everything remains flat and still in this reclusive space, which at the same time keeps in touch with the sky through a multitude of slender sources, deployed as either processional cues or accents to the funerary rite. Solitary pools of light relieve the funereal atmosphere with glimmers of the same washed-out hue – an image that merges being with non-being, and where life endures amid death. The disruption of brooding is especially touching at the chapel's main focus, where two adjacent yet differently angled rooftop chutes guide soft washes of natural light and, at times, sunbeams onto the altar and catafalque.

Above Overall view from the north; *top* Plan

Vestibule

Entrance to the main chapel

Pulpit

Skylit gallery wall

View across nave to the east wall, with its toplit recess, and gallery light slot at upper right

Adjacent light shafts in ceiling, above altar and catafalque

Detail of toplit recess

Skylit façade and sunlit tree

Mood of silent introspection

TAPIOLA CHURCH
TAPIOLA, FINLAND, 1965
BY AARNO RUUSUVUORI

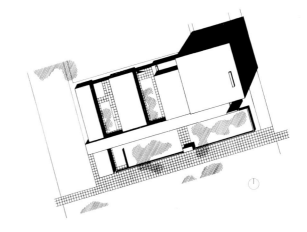

To construct a refuge of silence in this busy forest town, Aarno Ruusuvuori's church is withdrawn behind layers of wall and secluded gardens. Rising from this staged retreat is a sanctuary wrapped in folds of raw concrete, their surfaces tinged by delicate colours of sky and weather. The void within is more forsaken, for here there is nothing present but walls that have been totally stripped of iconography and colour. But there is a vital point to this absence, for, while physically emptied, the faded tones and static geometry make one aware of a slight living pulse in the play of light over the uneven concrete, and on coarse LECA (light-expanded clay aggregate) blocks that flicker with variations of grey. Compensating further for the bleakness are three dramatic beams of light from different sources. The majority of illumination is aimed to the altar from behind the seated congregation, its current filtered and focused by a clerestory grill, which tempers glare while directing light to the liturgical centre. Adding minor notes to the metaphysical presence, and helping to make the vacancy bearable, is a small amount of zenithal light from a rooftop slit above the altar, and again over the baptismal font to exalt its role and draw people into the church.

Above View of the altar wall from the west; *top* Site plan; *below* Longitudinal section, looking north

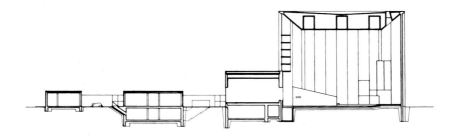

Skylight above altar

Baptismal font

Detail of sacristy

Gentleness amid emptiness

VARDÅSEN CHURCH
ASKER, NORWAY, 2003
BY TERJE GRØNMO

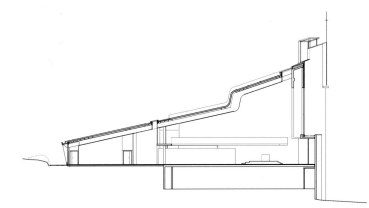

Sanctifying and drawing all eyes to the altar wall is light that arrives from two directions: from above through a rooftop slit, and from below through openings that dissolve the plane where it meets the floor and, like cross-hairs, converge onto a vertical slit behind the altar. Setting the mood is a grey backdrop of concrete walls, divested of all decoration but light that glances over their texture. Complementing this tonal key are a slightly darker grey floor and a slatted ceiling, along with occasional woodwork that tempers the absence by warming it where it is brought

into contact with people. The near extinction of colour arouses a slight anxiety, placing us in an emptiness of space that is tranquil yet deserted, leaving us starkly alone – a feeling intensified by the thinning down of material furnishings, from altar and pews to railings and lamps. But this palpable void is at the same time softened by the extraordinary gentleness and delicacy of things – creating a solitude that people are able to savour and enjoy, while at the same time shifting perception from outward to inward, and to a kind of seeing not done with the eyes.

Above Gallery with parish at left and church at right; *top* Transverse section, looking north

Above, left to right Detail at the northeast corner of the church; overall interior view from the southwest; altar; glimpse of the church from the entrance hall; *top* Gallery

North aisle from the east

South aisle with cloister doors at right

South aisle from the east

North aisle from the west

Mystical intensity of grey and violet penumbras

BENEDICTINE ABBEY
MARIAVALL, SWEDEN, 1995
BY HANS VAN DER LAAN

The exquisite feeling of silence inside Hans van der Laan's abbey resonates with the northern sky, while directly expressing a spiritual grace. It is not the building's strict and archaic forms, however, that provoke this strange evocative power, but rather another, second reality that has been allowed to emerge: a melancholy grandeur of soft penumbras and blurry light. Each humble material, in a world of simple things, is aimed at forging an atmosphere of holy emptiness and contemplative solitude: a grey concrete structure infilled with sober cement blocks; walls finished with modest and untreated planks of wood; and ceilings clad with similar planks that have been painted a heavenly blue. Rays of light that enter the voids from a limited number of small, square windows gradually spread from room to room, to slowly dim and fade into darkness before our eyes. Amid this loneliness of things in a barren space, and its infinite spectrum of greys and violets, light derives an enchanted yet mysterious stillness.

View of nave and altar from the west

Ground-floor corridor

End of upper-floor corridor

Upper-floor corridor with cell walls of wooden planks

Entrance to cell

Cell interior

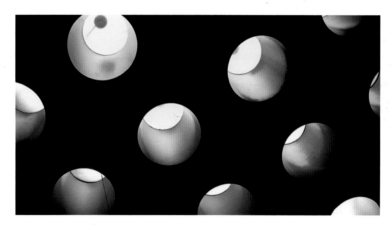

Rautatalo Office Building, Helsinki, Finland, 1955, by Alvar Aalto

8
DIFFUSION

The widespread distribution and softened glare of
scarce natural light

The overriding challenge of natural light for Nordic architects is its rarity. Even during the summer the intensity of light remains weak, diluted by low angles of incidence and a lengthy passage through the atmosphere. Over the course of the long, dark winter, the sun barely peeks above the horizon and remains in the south, so that all direct light arrives from virtually one direction at around noon. The practical implications of this pattern are profound, for, as Juha Leiviskä has observed, 'Light admitted from the south is the only possible source over the winter at northern latitudes.'[63]

blades, troughs and conduits added precision to the management of light and guided radiation as a flowing substance, while eliminating glare by diffusing the rays through a series of reflections. With its internal mass deeply hollowed to siphon light, an entire building that is closed to weather could be inwardly lit by the total available output of sunlight.

Pioneering this conception of architecture as an optical instrument was Alvar Aalto, whose seminal forms have been widely copied but rarely surpassed. Among his first and most daring achievements in maximizing northern light is the Paimio Sanatorium (1933; p. 21), in Finland, whose

Malmö City Library, Sweden, 1999, by Henning Larsen

Rødovre Library, Denmark, 1969, by Arne Jacobsen

Architectural methods to harness Scandinavia's meagre light began to emerge in the 1920s and '30s. The aim was to control and make use of daylight as a limited resource, while minimizing heat loss in an arctic climate, and to do this in a manner that retained an intimate contact with nature. The simplest technique that satisfied these needs was the moulding of the building's overall mass in response to the course of the sun, stretching and folding the envelope into carefully directed channels that would behave as funnels. The perimeter thus becomes a tool for catching and distributing light from very specific parts of the sky. These profiles were sculpted in both plan and section, and worked into rooflines and walls to capture low angles of light, and then convey that illumination to the innermost rooms of a building. Hydraulically shaped baffles,

openness reflects in part the accepted treatment for tuberculosis in the early twentieth century – exposing patients throughout the day to ample amounts of sunlight and fresh air. But Aalto carried this therapeutic aim beyond merely increasing fenestration. He broke the building down into narrow wings that were fanned out to the solar course, with slightly varied orientations according to their 'specific requirements of sun and view'.[64] The most crucial of these wings was the patients' ward, which was compressed into a thin block, highly porous to light and air, and given a prominent site at the southernmost edge of the complex. To subtly emphasize the morning sun when patients awake, the wing was bent slightly east of south, and the windows shifted asymmetrically to magnify early sunlight while lessening the stronger light of the afternoon. Ceilings were bevelled to increase the scope of gathered sky, further enhancing the capture of light. To escape the shadow of the patients' ward, the commons wing was set back to the north and entirely glazed along its south face, while the floor above the dining room was cut away to expose the full depth of the space to winter sunshine.

Aalto's exploitation of the roof as a complementary light source originated in the conical skylights that appear in both his Turun Sanomat Building (1929), in Turku, Finland, and Viipuri Library (1935), in Vyborg, Russia. These circular cells, which recur in most every Aalto building

derfully subtle detail, the drum's bottom edge was rounded off to perceptually soften the brightness contrast between drum and ceiling, and, as Aalto pointed out, to attain 'better light distribution'.[65]

Beyond their practical necessity and superb illumination, conical skylights offered Aalto a vehicle for poetic expression and formed what he called 'a celestial superstructure, crowded with suns that illuminate the sides with an even light'.[66] In their low veil of diffuse light, it is also possible to see a metaphoric link with the atmospheric Nordic sky – an image fostered by the soft glow and delicate colours of the orbs, as well

Lund Konsthall, Sweden, 1957, by Klas Anshelm

Høje-Taastrup High School, Denmark, 1981, by Henning Larsen

and are particularly elegant in the clusters over the Rautatalo Office Building (1955; p. 202) and the library for the National Pensions Institute (1956; p. 210), both in Helsinki, derived from studies of their optic behaviour. Each conical drum was dimensioned and shaped to diffuse falling light by a series of reflections, and then scatter this illumination off bevelled curves to the room below – a performance explored in Aalto's famous sketches for the Viipuri Library. In the same way that physicists draw flowing light, Aalto used spreading lines to study the paths of incident rays, showing how radiation was caught within the drums and then widely dispersed to land upon books from many directions. Potential glare was further reduced by dimensioning the drum height to intercept every solar angle up to its summer zenith. In a won-

as by their circular shapes and clustered grouping. While appearing grey under overcast weather, on clear days the skylights directly exposed to sun are tinged pale yellow, complementing those in the shade that are painted blue. Reconstituted overhead are the spectral components of the sky outside. Although architects throughout Scandinavia continue to employ Aalto's circular roof lights, their perfection has left little room for improvement, apart, perhaps, from the 'oblique cupolas' invented by Klas Anshelm to gently illuminate his Malmö Konsthall (1976; p. 214), or the extruded tubes by which Arne Jacobsen delivered zenithal light to the Rødovre Library (1969; opposite).[67]

The most eloquent device in Aalto's repertoire is the light-catching 'scoop', which was shaped to snare illumination from the horizon.

Rødovre Town Hall, Denmark, 1956, by Arne Jacobsen

Moulded and bent into a kind of periscope, the scoop was able to capture low angles of light and deflect these rays down into a room, and often further down to lower floor levels. In its rising gesture to reach for the sky, a scoop can utterly transform the silhouette of its building and become a source of architectural identity. Its embodiment of a specific climate, latitude and solar course brings architecture into accord with its setting, which is no longer defined solely in physical terms, and thereby helps people to concretely grasp their place in the world.

To adapt his scoops to diverse architectural functions and sites, Aalto invented a wide array of topologically varied shapes and maximized their light conduction with a smooth, white finish. A modest example is Seinäjoki Library (1965), in Finland, whose setting required that the reading room face south. To collect light for this room, while tempering sun, a south-facing scoop was placed overhead and protected outside by horizontal louvres, with its volume rendered convex in plan and concave in section to widen the arc of gathered sky and then bounce this illumination vertically down and back to the book stacks. In order to balance illumination in the sunken reading space and to throw some light onto the circulation desk, a bevelled channel was opened in the opposite direction to the north sky.

The collection of scarce light is particularly expressive in Aalto's Rovaniemi Library (1968), also in Finland, where a masterful series of large funnels fan out to a wide swathe of northern sky, maximizing the soft diffuse light that the architect thought essential to a place of books. While other spaces were packed into a rectilinear bar, the reading room rises from this base to form huge, almost ocular openings. Separated and fingered with walls between, the five funnels take slightly different segments of sky, deflecting some light back to the stacks and the remainder to reading areas below. The fan-shaped volume, a recurring motif in Aalto's libraries, is analogous to the edges of leaves and flower petals, which unfurl to gather more light. Illuminating other parts of the plan are circular skylights and smaller, south-facing scoops, which bathe various rooms with their own distinct character of light, while maintaining an emphasis on the reading room as the soul of the library. The drawings made for this library, which are among Aalto's finest, convey how every part of the section contributes to a search for light at the Arctic Circle.

Aalto's most exhaustive and sculptural treatment of the roof as a light source occurs at the Nordjyllands Art Museum (1972; p. 30), about which he observed: 'Light has the same significance for an art museum as acoustics for a concert hall.'[68] Covering the building is an assortment of scoops, each of whose optic behaviour is determined by the needs of its gallery below. Over the eastern, open-plan galleries are long, back-to-back scoops,

Suna School, Espoo, Finland, 1985, by Järvinen & Airas

sectionally carved like double-concave lenses and positioned to extend half-above and half-below the roof plane – but not equally, as the north-facing curves are slightly larger and higher to increase their proportion of diffuse light. The scoops span the space without intermediate support, shedding an even illumination throughout the room. Other devices take different shape, including a hybrid device that combines a large, high scoop, whose role is to collect horizontal rays and bend them down 90° to a hallway-cum-gallery, with a smaller, inverted scoop beneath, which intercepts a portion of falling light and diverts it into adjacent galleries. Most elaborate are the tiered scoops above the central hall, whose curves

take the light admitted from stepped clerestories and soften the rays while dispersing them over the exhibits below. Augmenting the light caught by the scoops are rooftop reflections from aluminium and enamel sheeting, seasonally enhanced by snow and sheets of shimmering water, exploiting the entire roof as a source of illumination.

Some of Aalto's light collectors were so large that they virtually encompassed the buildings they serve, moulding the silhouette into a single, optic idea. The dual needs of lighting and acoustics in the twin lecture rooms of the Helsinki Institute of Technology (1964; pp. 10, 11), for instance, led to a radial form whose sloping roof is porous to sunlight and merges into a canted wall at the rear of each hall. Below the tiered skylights are scoops that consist of blades, resting on concrete frames, with their cavities curved in both plan and section to gather a vast arc of sky and then diffuse this light before spreading it over the room below. Solar rays enter only after several reflections, and illumination is directed forward to the stage, as well as back to the seating. A similar theme dominates Aalto's church at Riola di Vergato, Italy (1978; p. 16), but here the section is orientated north to collect a soft, meditative light and minimize exposure to sun, allowing the scoops to spread wide open. Tiers of troughs reiterate the overall shell, and split the illumination by aiming a portion directly into the south of the nave, while deflecting the rest to the opposite side, thus balancing light in the room.

The paradigm of architecture as a light-catching instrument continues to be reinvented by other architects, generally through a language free of sinuous curves. At the Lund Konsthall (1957; p. 205), in Sweden, Klas Anshelm tapped the entire sky with a ring of inwardly sloping roofs of frosted glass. A related but now centrifugal idea was deployed by Henning Larsen at the Høje-Taastrup High School (1981; p. 205), near Copenhagen, lifting the solid slope of the roof off the classrooms and folding it back on itself three times in plan, to form a scoop that outwardly pans the full horizon. In doing so, the roof becomes a tertiary source of light that is bounced into three different floor levels. A circumferential device reappears in the smaller, inward-facing clerestory of Larsen's Gentofte Central Library (1985; below), which catches every angle of sky and is wrapped around a flat plane, riddled with circular roof lights. Contributing another dimension to this typology was Bernt Nyberg's Klockarebackens Chapel (1972), in Höör, Sweden, its perimeter skylights augmented by aluminium foil to illuminate the rough brick walls from inside, and make the introverted room feel aedicular and almost outdoors.

No architect since Aalto has attacked the scarcity of light – that old and urgent problem of Scandinavian architecture – with the boldness and imagination of Juha Leiviskä. Unfortunately, two of his greatest achievements in this regard remain unbuilt. At the Kajaani Art Museum (1988), in Finland, the challenge appeared deceptively simple, according to its architect: 'The exhibition areas were mainly lit by daylight, which was taken from the south, the only possible direction at this latitude. No sunlight, however, was allowed to shine on the inside walls.'[69] To overcome this, Leiviskä designed a chain of hexagonal galleries, illuminated by complementary scoops that were aimed south to capture and share the low sunshine. All of the devices were concave in section, and dimensioned to ensure that only reflected light reached galleries, but they varied in plan from concave clerestories to convex bands fed by high windows. Collectors were tiered to avoid shading one another, and to gather light throughout the day. Leiviskä's National Museum of Art (1994), proposed for Tallinn,

Gentofte Central Library, Copenhagen, Denmark, 1985, by Henning Larsen

Estonia, was equally impressive. Gently terraced to follow the sloping terrain, the building was to be illuminated by 'an overhead lighting system … used to give lighting that is rich in nuances and variations'.[70] This idea was worked out in sectional drawings, including one that studied the variety of angles taken by light as it was bounced into the galleries.

The daringly stepped skylights of Aalto and Leiviskä, along with the bilateral illumination of Gunnar Asplund's Göteborg Law Courts (1937), in Sweden, and Käpy and Simo Paavilainen's Olari Church (1981; pp. 2, 218), in Espoo, Finland, illustrate how the traditional clerestory has been adapted to highly directional Nordic light. But if this sort of device could illuminate a building's full depth, why couldn't it be expanded by extruding the section east and west? This possibility was explored by Sverre Fehn at his linear museums at Alvdal (1996; p. 64) and Ørsta (2000), both in Norway, where south-facing galleries were stretched into a long bar running east–west. Half-buried in a mountain slope, the sole openings of the latter's section are south-facing windows and clerestories that illuminate the entire plan, augmented by interior windows that share light with more enclosed rooms.

Also based on a daylit spine with a loosely bent sectional extrusion is Järvinen & Airas's Suna School (1985; p. 207), in Espoo, Finland, where the walls respond to terrestrial conditions and skylights twist to trap the morning sun when school is in session. 'The skylights were cut for the south sun,' says architect Kari Järvinen, 'and were angled southeast to get the morning light. Children come to school at about eight o'clock and leave at one or two, so the morning light is more important than that of the afternoon. Here I wanted every bit of sunlight I could get.'[71] The notion of rotating light-trapping elements to transcend site restrictions reappears in different guise in KHR Arkitekter's Hedorfs Residence Hall (2010), in Copenhagen, where multiple scoops emerged from the wall to catch tangential light from the street and draw it into the dormitory units.

The canyons and cores of Henning Larsen's designs merge light collection with spatial centres where human actions of fundamental importance occur. The existential value of these axes, both horizontal and vertical, is evident in the skylit interior 'streets' and courts of Larsen's Copenhagen Business School (1989; p. 26), as well as in the helical stair at the Ny Carlsberg Glyptotek Addition (1996; p. 92), also in the Danish capital. It is not the outward mass, but rather its light-filled voids, brightened by a white finish, which identify each building and make it memorable. Analogous is the atrium of the IT University of Copenhagen (2004; p. 222), also by Larsen, which forms a vessel into which daylight rains to illuminate its stairs, galleries and cantilevered, tray-like rooms. Extending this genre vertically is KHR Arkitekter's Kongens Nytorv

Station (2002; below), for the Copenhagen Metro, where daylight filters down through a shaft that is open to the sky, past escalators and landings to brighten the platform 22m underground.

The coalescence of street and light was compressed by Jokela & Kareoja into a three-storey slot, which runs along the north perimeter of their Government Office Building (1992; p. 224), in Rauma, Finland. This tall crevice, open to the sky, directs zenithal light onto walkways and stairs, while the blank north wall functions as a reflector, bouncing some of the rays back into the offices. The building clearly reiterates two basic themes in the Nordic pursuit of scarce natural light, beginning with the seminal role of a building section cut north-to-south along the meridian – confirmed by architect Olli-Pekka Jokela's comment that 'the section

The same tactic became a source of wispy beauty in Arne Jacobsen's elegant railings and mullions, risers and treads, which were pushed deliberately into the light-deluged vestibule of Rødovre Town Hall (1956; p. 206), and into the east end of the National Bank of Denmark (1971; pp. 149, 184). Complementing the practical value of maximizing the flow of weak light is the poetic value of expressing that light's inherent delicacy. Conveying much the same message is the reading room of Malmö City Library (1999; p. 204), by Henning Larsen, where a thin layer of stairs and bridges, study carrels and reading areas, screens a huge glass wall. As illumination filters through the white steel webbing, its backlit members appear more slender than they actually are, and largely melt into the light streaming through them.

Kongens Nytorv Station, Copenhagen, Denmark, 2002, by KHR Arkitekter

is most important in all of our buildings, and is the most important drawing'.[72] Equally significant is the minimizing of all obstructions to incoming light by thinning down stairs, railings, mullions and frames, while utilizing interior windows to borrow and spread illumination. Jokela & Kareoja's reduction of barriers to light brings us back to the Göteborg Law Courts, where Gunnar Asplund filtered light from the courtyard through a section of habitable space. In order to ease, rather than hinder, this flow, columns and banisters were gracefully thinned, and intervening volumes, from the elevator shaft to water basins, were dissolved with narrow frames and transparent glass.

Reference library

NATIONAL PENSIONS INSTITUTE
HELSINKI, FINLAND, 1956
BY ALVAR AALTO

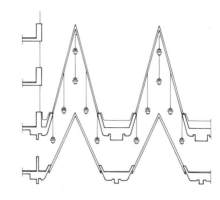

This icon of Finland's welfare state is filled with tools to siphon and share natural light – from its U-shaped mass, cut away to the south, and the cylindrical skylights of the reference library, to the mirror-like finish of the corridors, and the cracks and screens of interior walls. Most marvellous of all are the four 'crystal skylights', as Aalto christened them, above the main hall. Rising 12m high to catch the low winter sun, these steeply pitched glass volumes ricochet light down and into a four-storey space, including a glass-roofed corridor nested within the prisms themselves. Acting as great crystalline lenses, the glass sheets dispense illumination to every part of the room below. The double layers reduce heat loss and condensation, while providing a weather-free zone for lamps, allowing artificial illumination to be mixed with the ebbing and flowing sky, and ensure that, even in winter, zenithal light is shed on the innermost core of the building.

Above Skylit and sunlit conical skylights; *top* Transverse section of crystal skylights; *below* Section through the main hall, looking northwest

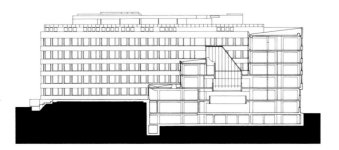

Exterior of crystal skylights

Upward view to crystal skylights over the main hall

Oblique cupolas

MALMÖ KONSTHALL
MALMÖ, SWEDEN, 1976
BY KLAS ANSHELM

The museum's entire roof is a honeycomb structure, porous to light. Complementing the single, north-facing lantern is a continuous grid of cellular voids, whose funnel-like shapes disperse soft light over the changing exhibits below. The breadth of illumination delivered by over five hundred sources, each framing the sky and streaked by sun, falls onto a primitive floor of unplaned wooden planks, making the large and unadorned gallery seem virtually outdoors. The shadowless light from the 'oblique cupolas', each performing, in architect Klas Anshelm's words, like 'the reflector in a work lamp', derives from their northward tilt and a section moulded to intercept all direct sun. The cell's uppermost metal collar increases reflections of sky and bulbs, while the lower and slightly bowed faces are painted white to gently spread illumination, casting an even glow that sparkles with faintly reflected sunspots.

Restroom window

Exhibition hall from the east

North wall of the exhibition hall

Upward view of oblique cupolas

Oblique cupolas with blending of direct sun, reflected sun and diffuse skylight

Exterior detail of the southwest corner

OLARI CHURCH
ESPOO, FINLAND, 1981
BY KÄPY AND SIMO PAAVILAINEN

One challenge posed by the hillside site was how to block southerly sun and street noise, while at the same time maximizing diffuse light from the quiet north side of the church. To resolve this dichotomy, a solid wall was placed to the south, with its palisade bent, broken and incised at intervals to admit indirect washes of sky and undistracting slivers of sun. Most illumination arrives from the north through a typically Finnish staggered section, with a window band, stepping up to a huge clerestory, which showers soft light onto the sanctuary's white finish. Balancing the illumination is a long, hooded monitor, immediately above the closed south wall, its scoop aimed north to brighten the south half of the nave and ensure a consistent character of light throughout the room. Among the church's wonderful details to augment illumination is an Aalto-esque carving away of the ceiling where it meets either wall. As these long troughs fill with light, they perceptually corrode the supporting structure, making the ceiling appear to float and be ringed with a halo.

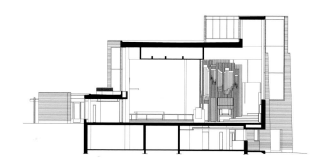

Above View of nave from the west; *top* Transverse section, looking east

Ceiling and light troughs at midway break in south wall

Upward view of ceiling and clerestories

Ceiling encompassed by light troughs

Midway shift of south wall and light troughs

Upward view of northwest corner of clerestory

Cantilevered drawers

IT UNIVERSITY OF COPENHAGEN
COPENHAGEN, DENMARK, 2004
BY HENNING LARSEN

Conceived as two parallel bars aligned roughly north to south, and containing between them a glazed atrium, architect Henning Larsen's design for this building maximizes illumination at its centre. Horizontal and vertical light mix together in the five-storey plenum, and then laterally spread to bordering rooms through open galleries, corridors and interior windows. The most striking agent in this dispersal is a series of white meeting rooms stuck into the traffic of light. Cantilevered like transparent 'drawers', varied in size and pulled out to differing lengths, these small cubes absorb some light while deflecting the remainder off their glazing and smooth, white profiles. During winter, the brief south sun is fully captured by the atrium as successive drawers filter, rather than block, the light as it streams through one room after another.

Above View of atrium from north; right Transverse section, looking north

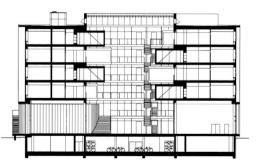

West side of atrium

Conference room

View between conference rooms to atrium

Gallery between atrium and classrooms

GOVERNMENT OFFICE BUILDING
RAUMA, FINLAND, 1992
BY JOKELA & KAREOJA

Stretching east and west along the bank of a scenic canal, this linear building is shaped to maximize south light on the side containing offices, while catching another dose of sun along the roof to illuminate its interior 'street'. The latter is achieved by a slot of space that is skylit over its entire length. Among the details used to enhance the capture of light is an extension of the north wall above the roofline, creating a rim and canted skylight to trap low angles of winter sun. Raining illumination is spread by reflections off the pure white finish, and bounced in part into the north glass edge of each office to balance the direct light from the south. To open the solid north wall to water views without diminishing its reflective power, the plane is cut away along its base and punctured above by small windows set at the eye level of workers inside, offering vistas and glimpses through a surface gleaming with light.

Above Gallery, with north wall beyond; *right* Transverse section, looking east

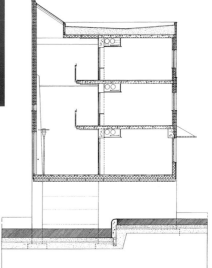

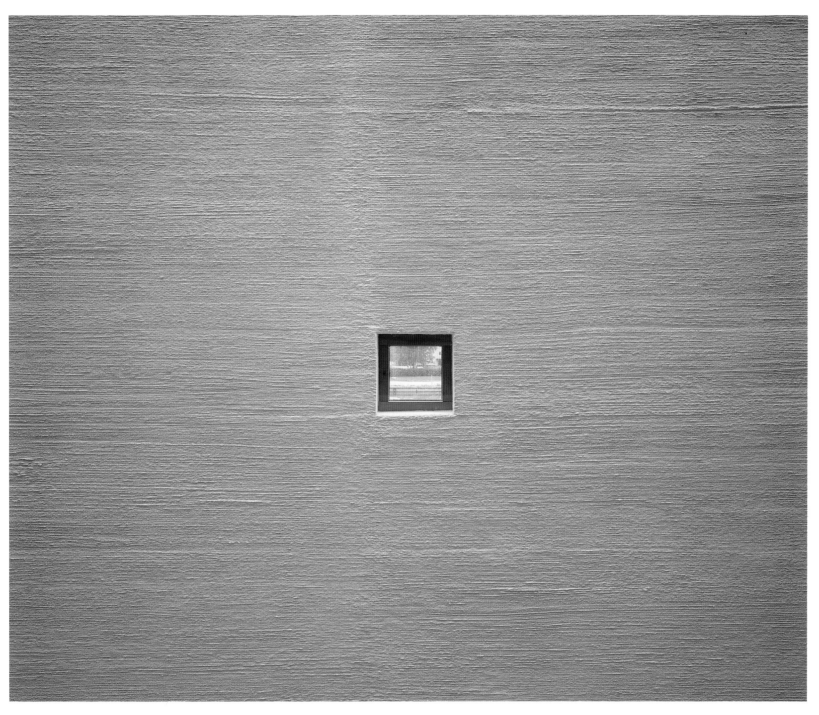

Above, left to right View of interior street and gallery from west; passage from staircase to gallery; two views of the staircase; *top* Detail of north wall

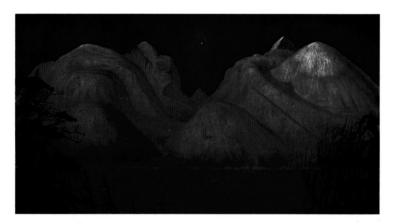

Winter Night in Rondane, 1914, by Harald Sohlberg

9

DARKNESS

The resonance of dark beginnings and arctic night
in shadowy spaces

The cult of light in Scandinavia overlies another, quite opposite tradition. As much as any force, it is the brooding darkness of winter night that identifies the North. For half a year the earth is cloaked in mysterious shadows and, apart from the faltering light at noon, a nocturnal mood unites the region. 'In the North,' writes Christian Norberg-Schulz in his aptly titled book *Nightlands*, 'it is only on winter nights that the sky becomes large, whole. Over the snow-covered earth, it vaults, saturated with a peculiar "dark light". Finally, it is cupola and firmament; a greater order emerges, and we see that the North is truly a midnight world.'[73]

Norway, were captivated instead of repelled by night phenomena, a fascination seen especially in the latter's *Winter Night in Rondane* (1914; p. 226). It should be no surprise that Kain Tapper, an artist drawn to elusive phenomena such as wind and morning mist, would also explore the secrets of darkness in his *Black Reliefs* some eighty years later. His works do not depict an absence of light, but abstract and reveal the endless black tones, vaguely coloured by moon and star, which enrich the night. A background of barely seen tones, burnt and rubbed into the surface, along with amorphous black shapes that one cannot quite make

Mortensrud Church, Oslo, Norway, 2002, by Jensen & Skodvin

Nørre Uttrup Church, Aalborg, Denmark, 1977, by Inger and Johannes Exner

The blackness of the Nordic night is evidently not a void but a place of wonder, containing its own subtle beauty of light and colour. Contributing to the faint radiance are strange ethereal happenings, which permeate into the waking hours and exist at the periphery of human awareness: dazzling stars fill the sky and coalesce into clusters; the aurora ripples with transparent curtains of green and pink light; and the ghostly luminescence of the moon, often encircled by halos and rings, takes over the role of the missing sun, shedding a silvery glow on the earth. Because darkness is such an unfamiliar subject of contemplation, especially for southerly cultures, it is helpful to consider the windows onto this elusive experience that artists have opened for us. Plein-air painters such as Eugène Jansson in Sweden and Harald Sohlberg in

out in the laminated wood, are set against rapid flecks of light – the kind we encounter when our eyes are shut.[74]

The same startling message – that darkness is never entirely devoid of light – has been conveyed in a different manner by James Turrell. In the *Dark Space* series, Turrell used non-light to widen the pupils of viewers, challenging their perception of the smallest possible quantity of illumination. Installations such as *Pleiades* (1983) and *Blind Sight* (1992) require at least twenty minutes for the eye to fully adjust to the dark, and lose impressions left on the retina, before detecting the pieces' extremely weak luminescence. As with Abstract Expressionist artist Ad Reinhardt's final *Black Paintings* of the 1960s, the viewer is not given forms modelled by light, but rather subliminal shades of blackness that are intended to stun and intrigue the eye, while increasing awareness of that dark vision Turrell calls 'the seeing from within'.

In addition to the long, dark winters, the heavy shadows of old peasant houses must have profoundly conditioned the Nordic mind.[75] Solidly built with logs and boards that were blackened over time by fire and smoke, these dim cabins were relieved by only a trickle of light through small openings cut in the walls. While early log huts were especially dark, their illumination drawn from a single door or smokehole, later cottages were given small, hatched windows that became glazed in

brighten and reveal a room covered above with layer upon layer of receding shadows. Gathered between the interlaced beams and dotted with light is a shade reminiscent of winter night, and conjures a mythical age when being emerged from nothingness.

A related darkness that invokes renewal is found in the traditional Finnish sauna. A faintly lit, womb-like space, built of heavy logs, the sauna's illumination comes solely from chinks between the timbers and small vents cut into the walls. The vaporous room is nocturnal in mood, a feeling intensified by tightly packed logs that have been darkened over

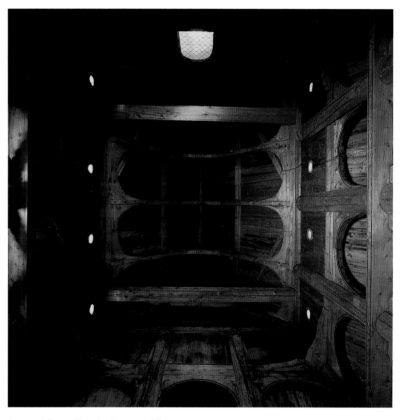

St Thomas Church, Vällingby, Sweden, 1959, by Peter Celsing

Borgund Stave Church, Norway, 12th century

the nineteenth century. These bare rooms of brownish-grey wood enhanced the velvety beauty of shadows and the feeble light allowed to enter. A more cavernous darkness developed within the Norwegian stave church, whose medieval gloom remains intact at the twelfth- and thirteenth-century churches at Urnes, Borgund (above), Kaupanger and Gol. Darkness even permeates into the woodwork itself, which was treated with tar for preservation, adding a sheen of blackness that palpitates and comes alive in the darkly glowing carvings around portals. Collecting inside these wood chambers is an exceptionally dense shade, pierced by only a few rays of light from tiny, round openings under the roof. As the human eye adapts to the dark, and a space that is only initially sensed through intense aromas of wood and tar, the dimness begins to slightly

time by soot and smoke, coating the walls with a glistening finish. As the first shelter built by settlers when constructing a new home, this dark vessel was the place where a family quite literally began its life. The gestative experience is re-enacted in the bathing ritual each time a person emerges naked from dark humidity into the cold light of day – a shock not unlike birth.

While contemporary saunas have lost much of their once-primordial character, these roots persist in Georg Grotenfelt's grass-roofed Huitukka Sauna (1982; p. 231), in Juva, Finland. With its 'small light apertures and a low door', Grotenfelt has observed, 'the sauna is a sacred place, an enclosed, dark and simple space for the cleansing of body and soul'.[76] The innermost chamber is pitch-black, with a few 'cracks' left in the construction, as Louis I. Kahn would say, 'to allow enough natural light to enter in to tell how dark it is'.[77] Duskiness envelops slender views of a shimmering lake, and offers barely enough illumination with which to perceive the surrounding black timbers salvaged from a drying barn. Made grimy and sooty from long exposure to heat and smoke, the woodwork absorbs the few entering rays to make the shade even thicker.

One of the first modern spaces to fully exploit the emotional power of Nordic darkness was Alvar Aalto's council chamber at Säynätsalo Town Hall (1952; p. 234), in Finland, which culminates the winding ascent to

surface, while at the same time making the bricks appear darker by contrast. Differences in the size of the bricks and courses, together with a deliberate unevenness contrived by laying the bricks without the use of a plumb line, give the walls a look of antiquity where the inherent darkness of each component is slightly varied by the light or shade caught on its facets. The premonitions outside are fully realized when a person steps into the church, to find the same bricks enclosing intensely dark rooms illuminated by a few cracks and holes in the wall. The continuous masonry of floor and vault, wall and pulpit, gives the shade a magnifi-

Islev Church, Copenhagen, Denmark, 1970, by Inger and Johannes Exner

Vatiala Cemetery Chapel, Kangasala, Finland, 1960, by Viljo Revell

its tower-like core. Several years later, in his closed brick churches, Peter Celsing began to freshly interpret the psychological impact of shade, using it to arouse a mystical feeling by shrouding the last few vestiges of light. Only a few spots of illumination were allowed to disturb the murkiness at Härlanda (1959; p. 236), in Göteberg, for instance, or at St Thomas (1959; p. 229), in Vällingby, both in Sweden, while glancing over rough bricks to create brooding volumes close to the earth.

Constructing equally tough but more shockingly primitive churches, also in Sweden, was Sigurd Lewerentz, who sought to give the darkness both a material and spatial dimension. Hard-baked bricks were employed for the inner and outer walls of St Mark's Church (1960), in Bjorkhagen, laid in a running bond with wide joints of white mortar to lighten the

cent wholeness, which is animated not only by roughness, but also by a ceiling structure that ripples and bows.

The burnt purplish bricks used at the church of St Peter (1966; p. 238), in Klippan, are even more rugged and dusky. Mortar joints were narrowed and recessed, throwing the bricks into relief and producing an inky texture that is then overlaid with the pure black lines of rails, lampposts and gutters. The calculated mood of desolation and old age, where the darkness attains both a physical and metaphysical presence, culminates in the sanctuary. Glinting in the dark are a few bare windows and ceiling slits, making shadows grow blacker. But then something miraculous occurs as a series of mysteries slowly take form in the blackened air, arising as pupils expand, initially as a baptismal font that opens a rent in the brick floor, its glistening black water overlooked by a huge seashell. After a time other uncanny things emerge, including the barely seen pulse of undulant vaults. Looming ahead at the centre of the nave is a huge column of rusted steel, its cross-beam spread to support the roof – suggesting a reddish-brown crucifix that bears the weight of the church, with undisguised allusions to the Passion of Christ.

The palpable darkness of Lewerentz's final churches is tied to an age-old ingredient of sacred space – shadows that are able to stir the subconscious, and lure the faithful into a state of reverie. There is an

sense' as 'non-being', but also in a 'positive sense' as an unformed state out of which being can be periodically renewed.[78] He goes on to argue that these dark settings are 'initiatory' in nature, for their loss of light offers churchgoers a 'symbolic death' equivalent to a *regressus ad uterum and a return to the pre-cosmogonic state'* – a regression that enables a 'new birth'.[79]

All of these archetypal encounters are condensed, and given forms at once archaic and modern, in three other remarkable churches dating from the 1960s: Huutoniemi Church (1964; p. 242) by Aarno

Huitukka Sauna, Juva, Finland, 1982, by Georg Grotenfelt

Malmi Church, Helsinki, Finland, 1981, by Kristian Gullichsen

immediate effect of infusing the church with mystery and awe, which speak to the soul with intimations of the numinous. But also present is a preformative and embryonic kind of darkness, a theme central to most religions, including Christianity, in that it conveys a negation out of which spiritual renewal is possible. Throughout architectural history the darkness protected in temples and churches has offered a place of primeval existence, where people can be immersed in shadows analogous to the womb before birth, the night before dawn and the cosmic night before creation. Visitors entering such a realm leave behind their previous existence and are invited to recreate themselves in a ritual act of rebirth. In his essay 'Shadows in Archaic Religions', historian Mircea Eliade points out that this kind of darkness is universally valued not only in a 'negative

Ruusuvuori and Vatiala Cemetery Chapel (1960; opposite) by Viljo Revell, both in Finland, and St Hallvard Church and Abbey (1966; p. 246) by Lund & Slaatto, in Oslo. Together with Lewerentz's last churches, these buildings constitute what are undeniably the major achievements of spiritualized darkness from the past century. The deep shade at Huutoniemi is continually invaded by a strange phosphorescence on dark LECA blocks, as the coarse texture picks up tiny particles of light to emit a faint molecular glow. Shadows in the vaguely pregnant vault over the Vatiala chapel embody Eliade's image of a darkness both nocturnal and gestative – a transitional state from which something new may come into being. Unlike the heavenly gesture of traditional church windows, the chapel's illumination is concentrated along the floor, its presence kept low and linked to side windows that open to nature. Attention is not drawn upward, but pulled horizontally out to light and water, and their implications for renewal, thereby helping the bereaved contemplate the meaning of death and the afterlife. As embryonic as the Vatiala chapel, but diametrically opposed in geometry, St Hallvard is one of Norway's most unforgettable expressions of dark light, and freshly interprets the stave-church concept of sacred space as a preformative darkness pierced by the faintest possible light. One can barely find one's way into the church, whose dark red bricks absorb most of the meagre light that leaks through the gaps and breaches in walls. Upon entering the central void, and only gradually over time, one grows aware of a strange apparition overhead, where the ceiling appears as an inverted vault that descends into the room itself. It seems as if a force is being exerted from the heavens, while at the same time forming an expectant curve in the womb-like hollow.

Few churches in later decades have so daringly explored darkness as a spiritual source. Among the exceptions in Finland is Kristian Gullichsen's Malmi Church (1981; p. 231), its weak illumination perceived as a series of penumbras that skim over the tactile brickwork. The faint brushings of light offer cues for human movement, culminating in the double plane of the altar wall, whose holiest spot lies at the border between darkness and half-light, where it mediates between non-being and being, symbolic death and renewal. Markedly different is the astral beauty of the Mortensrud Church (2002; p. 228), near Oslo, by Jensen & Skodvin. As illumination filters through its unmortared stone walls, infinite specks of light intermingle with the pulverized darkness to make the backlit stones even blacker, yet strangely twinkle.

The Scandinavian line of descent for spiritualized shade has fallen in Denmark to Inger and Johannes Exner. Their Islev Church (1970; p. 230) in Copenhagen retains a dark archaic beauty that is able to draw one into a trance. The almost imperceptible light enters from a continuous slit around the edge of the roof, its falling rays barely piercing the gloom and casting another layer of shade over the brickwork. Enveloping darkness throws attention to the slightly brighter zone of the altar, illuminated by a floor-level crack and glowing indentation above, which combine into a gentle beacon for the congregation – an inflection that becomes more pronounced in the pair's Nørre Uttrup Church (1977; p. 228), at Aalborg. Helping combat the *tenebrismo* in these exotic churches is a canopy of bare bulbs that are hung from the ceiling at a uniform plane just over the seating, their weightless glow counterpointing the massive dark walls. This sparkle offers a touching tribute to Scandinavia's winter skies and centuries of firelit peasant huts, comforting memories that are also stirred by the heavy and solid lamps of Sigurd Lewerentz; the industrial lamps of Simo and Käpy Paavilainen, as seen at St Michael's Church and Parish Centre (1988; p. 112), in Helsinki; and, most charming of all,

the lyrical clusters of golden lamps that float through the airy churches of Juha Leiviskä. In addition to their practical value in illuminating space and hymn-books at night, these lamps enhance the poetics of darkness. Their twinkling spots complete a familiar Nordic image of light that is perpetually fighting off darkness, giving the church not only a benediction, but also a firmament that expresses a basic truth.

Paralleling the mystique of darkness in certain Scandinavian churches, whose experience touches a primal nerve, are the less contemplative shadows of secular buildings that offer their own means of feeling at home in the dusky North. For practical reasons, this kind of darkness is generally limited to façades, producing a black body whose surface recedes on closer inspection to reveal hidden dimensions of shade, into whose secrets the eye can peer. The treasure chest of Peter Celsing's Bank of Sweden (1976; p. 18), for example, is dressed with black granite sheets, whose slabs have been vertically split to give each face a unique relief. Plates were assembled to alternate their concave and convex textures, and bring a mosaic-like shimmer to the blackness, with their surface depth amplified further by glints and shade in recessed windows that make the darkness seem to flicker from within. The nocturnal glow turns luxurious, even voluptuous, in the tilted and sheared monolith of Copenhagen's Royal Library (1999) by Schmidt Hammer Lassen. The so-called 'Black Diamond' is sheathed in smoothly polished black granite, allowing its canted surface to pick up unexpected images from the city and sky, as well as the harbour – fluid impressions that well up and then disappear in a black sheen that emanates from beneath its own contours.

Henning Larsen gains a harder and more cryptic impression with porous outer layers of metal that enwrap several office buildings in Copenhagen. The extremely murky skin of the Nordea Bank Headquarters (2000), its volumes clad with detached sheets of dark pre-oxidized copper, and of the Ferring International Centre (2002), wrapped in lacy black steel, float before a recessed shimmer of glass, producing a dimness that veils the sheen hiding behind. Their seductive elegance owes a debt to the aesthetic distillation of Mies van der Rohe's final buildings, which are reduced to nothing but sensuous dark cages, but his Danish offspring are far more gloomy and enigmatic, with inky tones that cloak rather than outline light, so as to wrap the utterly lucid forms in an aura of mystery.[80]

Among the rare Nordic architects who seek to bring shadows inside, where they infuse the space and substance of everyday buildings, is the Finnish firm Heikkinen-Komonen. Based upon an industrial palette of dim metal sheeting and porous screens that entrap shade, the total corpus of their Emergency Services College (1992) becomes imbued with the evocative force of winter night. This regional authenticity is developed through closely matched grey finishes, and the faint illumination of grey meshes to emphasize their murky, dream-like depths. Every neutrally coloured boundary, from metal panels and grilles to poured concrete and membranous glass, offers the eye yet another layer of materialized shade. By avoiding handicraft and being cleanly machined at every point, these minimalist buildings are stripped of overt aesthetic gestures, allowing their dimness to resonate, as the architects wished, with the grittiness of a soot-blackened factory or steel mill.

A related construct of muddy colours cloaked in shade is the Miesian box of Heikkinen-Komonen's Rovaniemi Airport Terminal (1992; p. 81), where neutral tones are vaguely tinted by changing hues of natural light, ranging from white or grey to blue or violet, and at times pink or yellow. The monotone voids are emotionally stirred by this almost imperceptible spectrum, producing a sumptuous feel that is paradoxically stark and empty. Contributing to the nocturnal mood is the night vision brought into play in this dim, grey space, emphasizing the rods, rather than the cones, of a human eye. As at night or fading dusk, the building itself is subdued and absorbed in something like smoke. These are exactly the faint and solemn hues that are treasured in Japan, where another culture of darkness developed that cultivates shade of every kind: the heavy shadows of farmhouses and palaces of the nobility, Zen temples and Shinto shrines; the weathered greys of the tea culture; and the contemporary silver-greys of architects Tadao Ando, Fumihiko Maki and Toyo Ito.[81] For passengers at Rovaniemi airport, anxious at the prospect of flight or awaiting those about to land, this kind of serenity offers a deep comfort.

Woodland Pool by Moonlight, 1881 by Hjalmar Munsterhjelm

Most marvellous of all the nocturnal touches at the Rovaniemi Airport Terminal, as well as at the Emergency Services College, is the shade caught above, and visible through, the suspended mesh ceilings. Darkness shrouds the black-painted ducts and conduits, dissolving away vertical limits while covering rooms with their own form of night. Turning amorphous and fading away,

this partly obscured layer of space arouses a drowsy kind of interest. Magnifying the experience are lamps hung within the interstitial darkness. We half-see their glowing orbs through a grey veil, and this fuzziness is further blurred as yellow light spills over the mesh from behind, spreading into soft halations. This by-now familiar Modernist detail has a certain authenticity in the North, where coronas are common in the arctic sky.[82] Darkness becomes something the eye can plumb and the mind explore – the same darker form of radiance that gives winter night its enchanting beauty.

SÄYNÄTSALO TOWN HALL
SÄYNÄTSALO, FINLAND, 1952
BY ALVAR AALTO

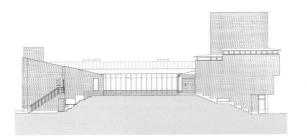

A labyrinthine path winds up and around the council chamber, whose secluded shade culminates the pregnant ground. Reduced illumination in the narrow staircase helps climbers prepare for the darkness to come, as does the filtration of light through a pine lattice and fringe of slats, a theme that returns in the final chamber, where timber baffles intercept light to create an intimacy that presses inward. Light is not set against shade, but is diminished and warmed to blend into darkness and infuse the space with perpetual twilight. The void seems caught in an in-between state, as if half asleep and waiting formation, expectant as a seed before germination or a child in the womb. As within the Finnish sauna, the shade at this town hall offers a regression from which something new and astonishing may emerge. As sight returns in the coloured darkness, one can gradually make out the celebrated fan-shaped trusses that support the roof, appearing as if from the depths of night and taking form before our eyes. Like coordinated fingers or arms, individual struts extend to support the roof, expressing the need for a repeated and shared renewal of self-government.

Above Wood baffles of the council chamber window; *top* Longitudinal section looking north; *right* Upper-level plan

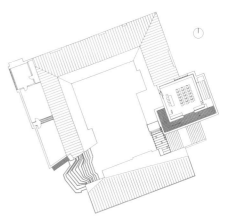

Above, left to right Looking back to the initial flight of stairs to the council chamber; second flight of stairs to the council chamber; door to council chamber at left; view back to the staircase; *top* Council chamber ceiling and roof trusses

Above, left to right Nave from the east; view across nave to the single column of the south aisle; main entrance; altar; *top* Wood-latticed recess of entrance

HÄRLANDA CHURCH
GÖTEBORG, SWEDEN, 1959
BY PETER CELSING

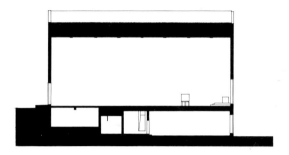

A living rather than petrified shade is produced at Härlanda by mixing seconds, or discarded bricks, into the standardized brickwork, and by the greyish-beige mortar joints that mingle into and modify the dark red hue of masonry. The heavy darkness within the closed church is relieved by scattered pools of light, positioned to accent key thresholds and liturgical features. Illumination from the few openings is cut down and muffled by glass lenses, and by wooden grilles that warm and sparkle around the entry. The most haunting penumbra is cast from a lone brick pillar along the nave, placed immediately in front of the only window on the south elevation – the side that receives all winter sun. In blocking the glare of incoming light, the backlit pillar creates a single, De Chirico-esque shadow, which exerts a strange metaphysical presence in the grim space. These atmospheric qualities were clearly a major concern of the architect, who commented wryly that the illumination sought in his churches was 'not just a suitable light for hymn-books'.

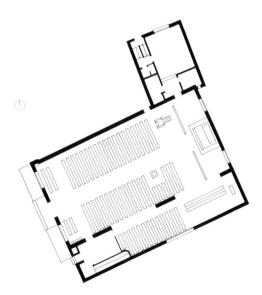

Above Altar window with glass lenses; *left* Plan; *top* Longitudinal section looking north

Miraculous things that slowly emerge in the dark

ST PETER'S CHURCH
KLIPPAN, SWEDEN, 1966
BY SIGURD LEWERENTZ

Invoking the oldest forms of human experience and sacred space, St Peter's Church plunges the visitor back into a world of darkness, causing one to blink and lose track of time, overcome with feelings that are barely conscious and recede far back in the memory. Inspired in part by an old brick factory in Helsingborg, where narrow sunbeams fell through the roof, Lewerentz's church is pierced by a few rays of light from small windows to the west and south, and several slits cut into vaults to mark the priest's journey from sacristy to altar. Underneath the heavy shade is a mild downward slope in the floor, as if sinking into the depths of the earth. This chthonic mood is reinforced by the baptismal font, which opens a crack within the pavement to make one aware of its hidden black pool and dripping water. Coming slowly into sight at the heart of the nave is a primitive cross of rusting steel, emerging like a cult object shrouded in darkness – a darkness that slows down space and time, and offers a matrix in which something miraculous may occur.

Above Baptismal font; *right* Plan

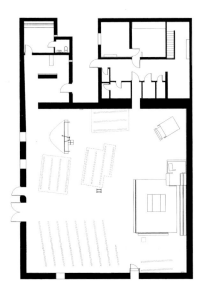

Above, left to right Passage from the sacristy to the church; skylight over the vestibule; conference-room
seating in the brick wall; parish hall windows; *top* View of the nave from the east

Detail of the steel column and beams

Skylights over the path between sacristy and altar

HUUTONIEMI CHURCH
VAASA, FINLAND, 1964
BY AARNO RUUSUVUORI

Hidden in boxes of bare concrete at this church in Finland is an unforeseen and eerie shade. Absorbing scant light is a dark inner lining of greyish-brown blocks of LECA concrete, whose slight but rapidly shifting tones give the wall a muted vibration, calmed at intervals by pitch-black joints. Some illumination comes from slits in the walls: a vertical slot near the entrance to guide arrival; a horizontal cut in the altar wall to mark the baptismal font; and a crevice formed by offset walls that allows a few rays to penetrate upward from below. Most illumination arrives from a window high in the west corner, which guides light over the altar wall while casting long shadows past the font and crucifix, altar and pulpit. Even under afternoon sun, the Caravaggio-like beams pierce without dispelling the shade. The most mesmerizing presence in this dusky room is also the subtlest – an interplay of glancing light with coarse masonry blocks. The combination of a granular surface and silky finish produces a texture that models and reflects light at once. These finely scaled modulations dim or brighten according to one's angle of view and the shifting character of Finnish light, which slants in obliquely to cast thousands of tiny shadows amid equally tiny glints, and cause the charcoal surface to sparkle. The resulting darkness is neither uniform nor stable, producing a phosphorescence similar to that of a starry sky or sea at night – a darkness mixing wonder with gloom.

Above Overall view from south; *below* Plan

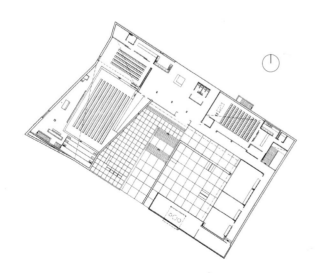

Above Late-afternoon sun on altar; *top* Mid-afternoon sun on altar wall

Baptismal font and slit window

Crucifix with altar wall beyond

Detail of pulpit and wall

Slit at entrance to church

Pulpit

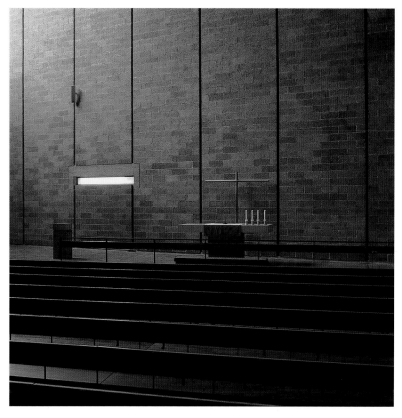

Nave and altar wall

Sidelit LECA masonry

Detail of altar and wall

ST HALLVARD CHURCH AND ABBEY
OSLO, NORWAY, 1966
BY LUND & SLAATTO

The mandalic church of St Hallvard, where a half-lit cubic perimeter surrounds a dark cylindrical core, draws one into thoughts of beginnings. The small amount of entering light is warmed by reflections off the archaic brickwork, and skims over the tactile walls, adding to the feeling of antiquity. Reached through dark slots of space, the innermost circular room is covered by the expectant curve of an ovoid roof. Despite the outward rationality of this geometric abbey, the unforgettable void at its centre is wholly irrational, forming a place that is dimly enigmatic and exceeds not only our visual grasp, but also our cognitive understanding. Within the heavy darkness of this hollow, making walls and floor all but invisible until one's eyes adjust to the faint light, and whose murky compression requires a force of will to enter, space feels emptied to make room for the uncanny presence of something pushing down from the sky.

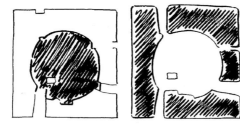

Above View of nave from the south; *top* Conceptual plans; *right* Plan

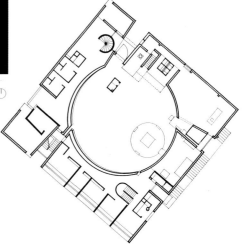

Bell and coloured shadows

Ambulatory

View into nave from the Maria chapel

View to nave from the southeast

Light niche over entrance

Upward view to convex ceiling

NOTES

1 While the term 'Scandinavia', strictly speaking, is limited to the countries of Norway, Sweden and Denmark, it is also often applied to Finland (and at times Iceland and the Faroe Islands), and it is in this more inclusive sense that the term is used in this book.

2 From an interview by the author with Kristian Gullichsen, 13 March 1996, in Helsinki.

3 *Northern Light* (Brooklyn Museum, New York; Corcoran Art Gallery, Washington, DC; Minneapolis Institute of Arts; Göteborg Konstmuseum, 1982–83); *The Mystic North* (Art Gallery of Ontario; Cincinnati Art Museum, 1984); *Dreams of a Summer Night* (Hayward Gallery, London; Kunstmuseum, Düsseldorf; Musée du Petit Palais, Paris, 1986); *The Light of the North* (Museo Nacional Centro de Arte Reina Sofía, Madrid; Museu d'Art Modern del MNAC, Barcelona; Listasafn Islands, Reykjavik; Nationalmuseum, Stockholm, 1995–96).

4 Alvar Aalto, 'The Trout and the Mountain Stream', in Göran Schildt, ed., *Alvar Aalto: Sketches*, trans. Stuart Wrede (Cambridge, Massachusetts: MIT Press, 1985): 96–98; Karl Fleig, ed., *Alvar Aalto. Volume I: 1922–62* (Zurich: Artemis, 1963): 49.

5 John House, 'An Outside View', in Leena Ahtola-Moorhouse, Carl Tomas Edam and Birgitta Schreiber, eds, *Dreams of a Summer Night: Scandinavian Painting at the Turn of the Century* (London: Arts Council of Great Britain, 1986): 22.

6 A more complete discussion of this discourse can be found in my earlier books *The Architecture of Natural Light* (London: Thames & Hudson, 2009) and *Masters of Light: Twentieth-Century Pioneers* (Tokyo: A+U Publishing Co, 2003).

7 Werner Haftmann, *The Mind and Work of Paul Klee* (London: Faber & Faber, 1954): 57–58.

8 From an interview by the author with Juhani Pallasmaa, 7 March 1996, in Helsinki.

9 From the poem 'Years Like Leaves', in Bo Carpelan, *Homecoming*, trans. David McDuff (Manchester: Carcanet Press, 1993): 111.

10 The interplay of ambient whiteness with small amounts of primary hues bears comparison with Le Corbusier's use of colour, aimed to intensify the white purity and perceptually activate certain forms, as well as with the colourations of De Stijl artist Piet Mondrian, and Gerrit Rietveld at his Schröder House (1925), in Utrecht. In the Dutch examples, flatly applied accents of black, red, blue and yellow were used to disengage various lines, planes and edges from one another, leaving their chromatic elements to float in a glowing white field.

11 'Light is the most important feature of the church,' Utzon explains. 'I provided white walls and white ceilings so that daylight, which is limited in Denmark for much of the year, is fully used and produces an intensity of light always greater than that outside.' From a discussion by the author with Jørn Utzon, 23 April 2002, at Can Lis, Mallorca.

12 Gaston Bachelard, *The Poetics of Space* (1958), trans. Maria Jolas (Boston: Beacon Press, 1969): 17.

13 From an interview by the author with Kari Järvinen, 14 March 1996, in Helsinki.

14 For a profound discussion of this image, see Chapter 5, 'Shells', in *The Poetics of Space*.

15 Canto 1, 'In the Beginning', in Elias Lönnrot, *The Kalevala*, trans. Keith Bosley (Oxford: Oxford University Press, 1989): 1–10.

16 Sigfried Giedion, *Space, Time and Architecture* (1941; Cambridge, Massachusetts: Harvard University Press, 1967): 622.

17 A perceptive essay on this subject is 'Elemental Matter in the Villa Mairea', in Scott Poole, *The New Finnish Architecture* (New York: Rizzoli, 1992): 18–27.

18 These vacant and dry details, where light melts away form with sfumato effects, recall the 'jug' extolled by Martin Heidegger in his essay, 'The Thing', which 'retain[s] its nature by virtue of the poured gift ... even though empty'. Heidegger, *Poetry, Language, Thought*, trans. Albert Hofstadter (New York: Harper & Row, 1971): 172.

19 Lönnrot, 8.

20 A similar perspectival shift was employed by Nordic painters in the early 1900s, especially Sweden's Gustaf Fjaestad, to bring wavery sheets of dark, icy water almost parallel with the canvas.

21 Bo Carpelan, *Room Without Walls*, trans. Anne Born (London: Forest Books, 1987): 76.

22 Although Umberto Boccioni's *Development of a Bottle in Space* (1912) was ostensibly the model for Pietilä's church, the fluttering lines of Giacomo Balla's paintings and drawings seem closer in spirit to the building's vibrantly calm energy and, apart from the floor plan, gestural restraint.

23 It is telling that Pietilä's competition entry was given the pseudonym 'Mica Moraine', and that during its conceptualization he recalls making 'imaginary sketches of the terminal moraine of a glacial flow', with 'sections and plans though not elevations of this crystalline phenomenon, this monstrous iceberg', envisioning from the outset a kind of 'ice architecture'. Reima Pietilä, *Pietilä: Intermediate Zones in Modern Architecture* (Helsinki: Museum of Finnish Architecture, 1985): 30.

24 Bruno Taut, 'Alpine Architecture' (1919), in Dennis Sharp, ed., *Glass Architecture and Alpine Architecture* (New York: Praeger, 1972): 124.

25 For instance, with regard to Kahn, the Salk Institute (1965) in La Jolla, California; the exterior façades of the Unitarian Church (1969) in Rochester, New York; and the hostels for the National Capital of Bangladesh project (1983), in Dhaka.

26 An accomplished pianist as well as architect, Juha Leiviskä developed a sensibility in which sight and sound are closely blended.

27 For an examination of the art of light in Japanese culture, see my book *Light in Japanese Architecture* (Tokyo: A+U Publishing Co, 1995).

28 The term 'primal image' is Gaston Bachelard's. 'Primal images, simple engravings are but so many invitations to start imagining again,' he contends. 'They give us back areas of being, houses in which the human being's certainty of being is concentrated, and we have the impression that, by living in such images as these, in images that are as stabilizing as these are, we could start a new life, a life that would be our own, that would belong to us in our very depths.' *The Poetics of Space*, 33.

29 American mythologist Joseph Campbell has argued that the universal meaning of the dark threshold stems from human birth. Campbell, *The Masks of God: Primitive Mythology* (Harmondsworth, England: Penguin, 1976): 61–62.

30 C. G. Jung, *Memories, Dreams, Reflections*, ed. Aniela Jaffé (New York: Pantheon, 1961): 269.

31 Gaston Bachelard, *Air and Dreams: An Essay on the Imagination of Movement* (1943), trans. Edith R. Farrell and C. Frederick Farrell (Dallas: Dallas Institute Publications, 1988): 43.

32 Ibid., 33.

33 Mircea Eliade, *The Sacred and the Profane: The Nature of Religion*, trans. Willard R. Trask (New York: Harcourt, Brace & World, 1959): 179–201.

34 Henry David Thoreau, *Walden* (1854; New York: Airmont, 1965): 38.

35 This same scenario reappears with great elaboration in Tadao Ando's Church on the Water (1988), in northern Japan.

36 Richard Wollheim, ed., *The Image in Form: Selected Writings of Adrian Stokes* (New York: Harper & Row, 1972): 47–48.

37 Ibid., 47.

38 As in the thick windows beloved by Louis I. Kahn, the halftones serve also a practical aim in reducing glare and the sharp contrast of sun and shade.

39 James Turrell, *Air Mass* (London: South Bank Centre, 1993): 26.

40 From an interview by the author with Olli-Pekka Jokela, 8 March 1996, in Helsinki.

41 Ibid.

42 Corinne Diserens, ed., *Gordon Matta-Clark* (London: Phaidon, 2003): 165.

43 Ibid., 178.

44 Tarjei Vesaas, *The Ice Palace* (1963); trans. Elizabeth Rokkan (London: Peter Owen, 2005): 47, 51.

45 Paul Scheerbart, 'Glass Architecture' (1914), in Sharp, 46, 52, 66.

46 Juhani Pallasmaa, ed., *The Language of Wood: Wood in Finnish Sculpture, Design and Architecture* (Helsinki: Museum of Finnish Architecture, 1987). Pallasmaa has been writing and lecturing about 'forest space' since the early 1980s.

47 For an account of Norwegian masters of timber architecture, see Beate Hølmebakk, ed., *Timberwork* (Oslo: Arkitekturforlaget, 2000).

48 *The Poetics of Space*, 187.

49 Interview with Kristian Gullichsen.

50 Henri Bergson, *Matter and Memory* (1896); trans. Nancy Margaret Paul and W. Scott Palmer (New York: Zone, 1988): 186, 205–7; Susanne K. Langer, *Feeling and Form: A Theory of Art* (New York: Scribner, 1953): 109.

51 For a fuller account of mobile and cinematic light in architecture see my books *Poetics of Light* (Tokyo: A+U Publishing Co, 1987): 137–95; *Light in Japanese Architecture*, 348–93; and *The Architecture of Natural Light*, 16–51.

52 Revised Standard Version, 1 John 1:5 and John 8:12.

53 Andrey Tarkovsky, *Sculpting in Time*, trans. Kitty Hunter-Blair (Austin: University of Texas, 1986): 63.

54 From an interview by the author with Juha Leiviskä, 3 March 1996, in Helsinki.

55 Owing to varying site conditions, Juha Leiviskä's orientation of slots differs slightly from church to church, and is often not precisely aimed south, which alters the moment of transfiguration by the entering sun. The slots at Myyrmäki Church run somewhat east of due south, for instance, emphasizing the time immediately before noon, while those at Männistö Church run somewhat west of south, admitting sunlight shortly after noon, with the liturgical emphasis coming instead from the ethereal colours produced as the sun reflects off patches of paint on the backside of the baffles.

56 Richard Kostelenetz, ed., *Moholy-Nagy* (New York: Praeger, 1970): 155–56.

57 From an interview by the author with Simo Paavilainen, 11 March 1996, in Helsinki.

58 Kirsi Leiman, ed., *Concrete Spaces: Architect Aarno Ruusuvuori's Works from the 1960s* (Helsinki: Museum of Finnish Architecture, 2000): 47.

59 *Masters of Light: Twentieth-Century Pioneers*, 236–53.

60 A profound examination of the necessity of silence, and its recent loss in the human world, is *The World of Silence* by the Swiss philosopher Max Picard. Picard, *The World of Silence* (1948); trans. Stanley Godman (Washington: Regnery Gateway Editions, 1988).

61 Daisetz T. Suzuki, *Zen and Japanese Culture* (Princeton, New Jersey: Princeton University Press, 1970): 284.

62 H. H. Arnason, *History of Modern Art* (New York: Abrams, 1986): 188.

63 Interview with Juha Leiviskä.

64 Fleig, 31; *Alvar Aalto, Paimio 1929–1933*, trans. Jonathan Moorhouse and Leena Ahtola-Moorhouse (Jyväskylä, Finland: Alvar Aalto Museum, 1976): n.p.

65 Fleig, 186.

66 Alvar Aalto, 'The Egg of the Fish and the Salmon', in *Architects' Year Book 8* (London: Elek Books, 1957): 138.

67 Aalto's glass prisms at the National Pensions Institute (1956) and Academic Bookstore (1962), both in Helsinki, can also be considered exotic tools used to collect and dispense zenithal light, in each case enhanced by carving away the building's south profile to avoid blocking the low winter sun.

68 Fleig, 210. The museum was designed in collaboration with Danish architect Jean-Jacques Baruël, who worked in Aalto's office during the 1950s.

69 Marja-Riitta Norri and Kristiina Paatero, eds, *Juha Leiviskä* (Helsinki: Museum of Finnish Architecture, 1999): 114.

70 Ibid., 168.

71 Interview with Kari Järvinen.

72 Interview with Olli-Pekka Jokela.

73 Christian Norberg-Schulz, *Nightlands: Nordic Building* (Cambridge, Massachusetts: MIT Press, 1996): 6.

74 Juhani Pallasmaa, ed., *Kain Tapper: Tombs in Wood* (Helsinki: Art Print, 1994).

75 This idea was suggested to me by Juhani Pallasmaa during a conversation in June 1995 in Helsinki.

76 Marja-Riitta Norri and Maija Kärkkäinen, eds, *An Architectural Present – Seven Approaches* (Helsinki: Museum of Finnish Architecture, 1990): 151.

77 Louis I. Kahn, 'Structure and Form', in *Forum Lectures* (Washington, DC: Voice of America, 1960).

78 Mircea Eliade, *Symbolism, the Sacred and the Arts*, ed. Diane Apostolos-Cappadona (New York: The Crossroad Publishing Company, 1988): 7.

79 Ibid., 7–8. See also *Poetics of Light*, 73–136; *Light in Japanese Architecture*, 100–35.

80 For instance, Mies van der Rohe's lithe structure of graphite-black steel at the Lake Shore Towers (1951) in Chicago, the dimly patinated bronze of the Seagram Building (1958) in New York, and the dark grey steel of the Bacardi Building (1961) in Santiago, Chile.

81 For an eloquent discussion of the Japanese penchant for darkness, see Jun'ichiro Tanizaki, *In Praise of Shadows* (1933); trans. Thomas J. Harper and Edward G. Seidensticker (New Haven, Connecticut: Leete's Island Books, 1977).

82 In cold, northern climates, aureoles are produced when banks of fog or mist glide before the sun, moon or stars, causing them to shine through a molecular medium. The clouds of tiny ice crystals that make up the fog or cloud refract passing light into a halo.

BIBLIOGRAPHY

Ahlin, Janne, *Sigurd Lewerentz: Architect 1885–1975*, trans. Kerstin Westerlund (Cambridge, Massachusetts: MIT Press, 1987).

Ahtola-Moorhouse, Leena, Carl Tomas Edam and Birgitta Schreiber, eds, *Dreams of a Summer Night: Scandinavian Painting at the Turn of the Century* (London: Arts Council of Great Britain, 1986).

Alvar Aalto, Paimio, trans. Jonathan Moorhouse and Leena Ahtola-Moorhouse (Jyväskylä, Finland: Alvar Aalto Museum, 1976).

Architects' Year Book 8 (London: Elek Books, 1957).

Arnason, H. H., *History of Modern Art* (New York: Abrams, 1986).

Bachelard, Gaston, *Air and Dreams: An Essay on the Imagination of Movement* (1943), trans. Edith R. Farrell and C. Frederick Farrell (Dallas: Dallas Institute Publications, 1988).

———, *The Flame of a Candle* (1961), trans. Joni Caldwell (Dallas: Dallas Institute Publications, 1988).

———, *The Poetics of Space* (1958), trans. Maria Jolas (Boston: Beacon Press, 1969).

———, *Water and Dreams: An Essay on the Imagination of Matter* (1942), trans. Edith R. Farrell (Dallas: The Pegasus Foundation, 1983).

Bak, Aase, ed, *Nordjyllands Kunstmuseum* (Copenhagen: Fonden til udgivelse af Arkitekturtidsskrift, 1999).

Bergson, Henri, *Matter and Memory* (1896), trans. Nancy Margaret Paul and W. Scott Palmer (New York: Zone, 1988).

Bjerke, Øivind Storm, *Edvard Munch and Harald Sohlberg: Landscapes of the Mind* (New York: National Academy of Design, 1995).

Brawne, Michael, *Jørgen Bo, Vilhelm Wohlert: Louisiana Museum, Humlebæk* (Berlin: Ernst Wasmuth, 1993).

Caldenby, Claes, *Sigurd Lewerentz: Two Churches* (Stockholm: Arkitektur Förlag, 1997).

Caldenby, Claes, Jöran Lindvall and Wilfried Wang, *Twentieth-Century Architecture: Sweden* (Munich: Prestel, 1998).

Campbell, Joseph, *The Masks of God: Primitive Mythology* (Harmondsworth, England: Penguin, 1976).

Carpelan, Bo, *Homecoming*, trans. David McDuff (Manchester: Carcanet Press, 1993).

———, *Room Without Walls*, trans. Anne Born (London: Forest Books, 1987).

Cassirer, Ernst, *The Philosophy of Symbolic Forms*, 3 vols., trans. Ralph Mannheim (New Haven, Connecticut: Yale University Press, 1953).

Davey, Peter, *Heikkinen & Komonen*, ed. Xavier Güell (Barcelona: Gustavo Gili, 1994).

Diserens, Corinne, ed., *Gordon Matta-Clark* (London: Phaidon, 2003).

Donnelly, Marian C., *Architecture in the Scandinavian Countries* (Cambridge, Massachusetts: MIT Press, 1992).

Dubos, René, *So Human an Animal* (New York: Scribner, 1968).

Dymling, Claes, ed, *Architect Sigurd Lewerentz*, 2 vols (Stockholm: Byggförlaget, 1997).

Eliade, Mircea, *Patterns in Comparative Religion*, trans. Rosemary Sheed (New York: Meridian, 1963).

———, *The Sacred and the Profane: The Nature of Religion*, trans. Willard R. Trask (New York: Harcourt, Brace & World, 1959).

———, *Symbolism, the Sacred and the Arts*, ed. Diane Apostolos-Cappadona (New York: The Crossroad Publishing Company, 1988).

Ferlenga, Alberto, and Paola Verde, *Dom Hans van der Laan: Works and Words* (Amsterdam: Architectura & Natura, 2001).

Fernández-Galiano, Luis, ed., 'Escandinavos Scandinavians', in *AV Arquitectura Viva 55* (1995).

Fjeld, Per Olaf, *Sverre Fehn: The Pattern of Thoughts* (New York: Monacelli Press, 2009).

———, *Sverre Fehn: The Thought of Construction* (New York: Rizzoli, 1983).

Fleig, Karl, ed., *Alvar Aalto: Volume I 1922–62* (Zurich: Artemis, 1963).

———, *Alvar Aalto: Volume II 1963–70* (Zurich: Artemis, 1971).

———, *Alvar Aalto: Volume III Projects and Final Buildings* (Zurich: Artemis, 1978).

Fonsmark, Anne-Birgitte and Mikael Wivel, eds, *Vilhelm Hammershøi 1864–1916: Danish Painter of Solitude and Light* (Copenhagen: Ordrupgaard, 1997).

Giedion, Sigfried, *Space, Time and Architecture* (1941; Cambridge, Massachusetts: Harvard University Press, 1967).

Grønvold, Ulf, *Lund & Slaatto* (Oslo: Universitetsforlaget, 1988).

Gutheim, Frederick, *Alvar Aalto* (New York: George Braziller, 1960).

Haftmann, Werner, *The Mind and Work of Paul Klee* (London: Faber & Faber, 1954).

Heidegger, Martin, *Poetry, Language, Thought*, trans. Albert Hofstadter (New York: Harper & Row, 1971).

Holmbom, Anna, ed., *Malmö Konsthall 1975–2005* (Malmö: Malmö Konsthall, 2005).

Hølmebakk, Beate, ed., *Timberwork* (Oslo: Arkitekturforlaget, 2000).

Hultin, Olof, ed., *The Architecture of Peter Celsing* (Stockholm: Arkitektur Förlag, 1996).

Ilvas, Juha, ed., *Akseli Gallen-Kallela* (Helsinki: Ateneum Publications, 1996).

Jones, Peter Blundell, *Gunnar Asplund* (London: Phaidon, 2006).

Jung, C. G., *Memories, Dreams, Reflections*, ed. Aniela Jaffé (New York: Pantheon, 1961).

Kahn, Louis I., 'Structure and Form', in *Forum Lectures* (Washington, DC: Voice of America, 1960).

Kaipia, Jouni, ed., *Concrete in Finnish Architecture*, trans. Pirjo Kuuselo (Helsinki: Museum of Finnish Architecture, 1989).

Kaiser, Lise, ed., *Henning Larsen* (Humlebæk: Louisiana Museum, 1999).

Kämäräinen, Eija, *Akseli Gallen-Kallela*, trans. Michael Wynne-Ellis (Helsinki: WSOY, 1994).

Kent, Neil, *The Triumph of Light and Nature: Nordic Art 1740–1940* (London: Thames & Hudson, 1987).

Kostelenetz, Richard, ed., *Moholy-Nagy* (New York: Praeger, 1970).

Langer, Susanne K., *Feeling and Form: A Theory of Art* (New York: Scribner, 1953).

Leiman, Kirsi, ed., *Concrete Spaces: Architect Aarno Ruusuvuori's Works from the 1960s* (Helsinki: Museum of Finnish Architecture, 2000).

Leiviskä, Juha, 'Juha Leiviskä', in *a+u 250* (July 1991): 48–128.

———, 'Juha Leiviskä', in *a+u 295* (April 1995): 6–139.

———, 'Juha Leiviskä', in *L'Architecture d'aujourd'hui* (October 1995): 53–85.

Lönnrot, Elias, *The Kalevala*, trans. Keith Bosley (Oxford: Oxford University Press, 1989).

Lopez, Barry, *Arctic Dreams* (New York: Scribner, 1986).

Lund, Nils-Ole, *Arkitekt Henning Larsen* (Copenhagen: Gyldendal, 1996).

Merleau-Ponty, Maurice, *Phenomenology of Perception*, trans. Colin Smith (London: Routledge & Kegan Paul, 1962).

Minnaert, Marcel, *The Nature of Light and Colour in the Open Air*, trans. H. M. Kremer-Priest (New York: Dover, 1954).

Møller, Erik, *Århus City Hall* (Copenhagen: Danish Architectural Press, 1991).

Møller, Henrik Sten, *Light and Life: Henning Larsen, the Man and the Architect* (Copenhagen: Politiken, 2000).

Monrad, Kasper, Björn Fredlund and Birgitta Schreiber, eds, *Lux del Norte, Llum del Nord: The Light of the North* (Madrid: Museo Nacional Centro de Arte Reina Sofía, 1995).

Monrad, Kasper and Karin Sidén, eds, *Nordiskt Sekelskifte: The Light of the North* (Stockholm: Nationalmuseum, 1995).

Morell, Lars, *Per Kirkeby: The Art of Building* (Copenhagen: Aristo, 1996).

Nasgaard, Roald, *The Mystic North* (Toronto: University of Toronto Press, 1984).

Nikula, Riitta, ed., *Erik Bryggman 1891–1955* (Helsinki: Museum of Finnish Architecture, 1991).

Norberg-Schulz, Christian, *Existence, Space & Architecture* (New York: Praeger, 1971).

———, *Genius Loci: Towards a Phenomenology of Architecture* (New York: Rizzoli, 1980).

———, *Lund & Slaatto: St Hallvard Kirke og Kloster* (Oslo: Arfo, 1997).

———, *Modern Norwegian Architecture* (Oslo: Norwegian University Press, 1986).

———, *Nightlands: Nordic Building* (Cambridge, Massachusetts: MIT Press, 1996).

Norberg-Schulz, Christian, and Gennaro Postiglione, *Sverre Fehn: Works, Projects, Writings, 1949–1996* (New York: Monacelli, 1997).

Norri, Marja-Riitta, ed., *Architecture in Miniature: Juhani Pallasmaa Finland* (Helsinki: Museum of Finnish Architecture, 1991).

Norri, Marja-Riitta, and Maija Kärkkäinen, eds, *An Architectural Present – Seven Approaches* (Helsinki: Museum of Finnish Architecture, 1990).

———, *Sverre Fehn: The Poetry of the Straight Line* (Helsinki: Museum of Finnish Architecture, 1992).

Norri, Marja-Riitta, and Kristiina Paatero, eds, *Juha Leiviskä* (Helsinki: Museum of Finnish Architecture, 1999).

Norri, Marja-Riitta, Elina Standertskjöld and Wilfried Wang, eds, *Twentieth-Century Architecture: Finland* (Munich: Prestel, 2000).

Pallasmaa, Juhani, *The Eyes of the Skin: Architecture and the Senses* (London: Academy Editions, 1996).

Pallasmaa, Juhani, ed., *Kain Tapper: Tombs in Wood* (Helsinki: Art Print, 1994).

———, *The Language of Wood: Wood in Finnish Sculpture, Design and Architecture* (Helsinki: Museum of Finnish Architecture, 1987).

Pearson, Paul David, *Alvar Aalto and the International Style* (New York: Whitney Library of Design, 1978).

Pettersson, Lars, *Suomalainen Puukirkko, Finnish Wooden Church* (Helsinki: Otava, 1992).

Picard, Max, *The World of Silence* (1948), trans. Stanley Godwin (Washington, DC: Regnery Gateway Editions, 1988).

Pietilä, Reima, *Pietilä: Intermediate Zones in Modern Architecture* (Helsinki: Museum of Finnish Architecture, 1985).

Plummer, Henry, *The Architecture of Natural Light* (London: Thames & Hudson, 2009).

———, *Light in Japanese Architecture* (Tokyo: A+U Publishing Co, 1995).

———, *Masters of Light: Twentieth-Century Pioneers* (Tokyo: A+U Publishing Co, 2003).

———, *Poetics of Light* (Tokyo: A+U Publishing Co, 1987).

———, *Stillness and Light: The Silent Eloquence of Shaker Architecture* (Bloomington, Indiana: Indiana University Press, 2009).

Poole, Scott, *The New Finnish Architecture* (New York: Rizzoli, 1992).

Quantrill, Malcolm, *Finnish Architecture and the Modernist Tradition* (London: E & FN Spon, 1995).

———, *Reima Pietilä: Architecture, Context and Modernism* (New York: Rizzoli, 1985).

Rasmussen, Steen Eiler, *Experiencing Architecture* (Cambridge, Massachusetts: MIT Press, 1962).

Reenberg, Holger, ed., *Heart: Steven Holl* (Ostfildern, Germany: Hatje Cantz Verlag, 2009).

Richards, J. M., *A Guide to Finnish Architecture* (New York: Praeger, 1967).

Schildt, Göran, *Alvar Aalto: The Decisive Years* (New York: Rizzoli, 1986).

———, *Alvar Aalto: The Early Years* (New York: Rizzoli, 1984).

———, *Alvar Aalto: The Mature Years* (New York: Rizzoli, 1991).

———, *Modern Finnish Sculpture* (New York: Praeger, 1970).

Schildt, Göran, ed., *Alvar Aalto: Sketches*, trans. Stuart Wrede (Cambridge, Massachusetts: MIT Press, 1985).

Sharp, Dennis, ed., *Glass Architecture and Alpine Architecture* (New York: Praeger, 1972).

Suzuki, Daisetz T., *Zen and Japanese Culture* (Princeton, New Jersey: Princeton University Press, 1970).

Svedberg, Olle, *The Architecture of Klas Anshelm* (Stockholm: Arkitektur Förlag, 2004).

Tanizaki, Jun'ichiro, *In Praise of Shadows* (1933), trans. Thomas J. Harper and Edward G. Seidensticker (New Haven, Connecticut: Leete's Island Books, 1977).

Tarkovsky, Andrey, *Sculpting in Time*, trans. Kitty Hunter-Blair (Austin: University of Texas, 1986).

Tempel, Egon, *New Finnish Architecture* (New York: Praeger, 1968).

Thau, Carsten, and Kjeld Vindum, *Arne Jacobsen* (Copenhagen: Arkitektens Forlag, 2001).

Thoreau, Henry David, *Walden* (1854; New York: Airmont, 1965).

Tuovinen, Anna, *Pekka Halonen 1865–1933* (Lapinlahti, Finland: Lapinlahden Taidemuseo, 1995).

Turrell, James, *Air Mass* (London: South Bank Centre, 1993).

Vad, Poul, *Vilhelm Hammershøi and Danish Art at the Turn of the Century*, trans. Kenneth Tindall (New Haven, Connecticut: Yale University Press, 1992).

Varnedoe, Kirk, *Northern Light: Nordic Art at the Turn of the Century* (New Haven, Connecticut: Yale University Press, 1988).

Vesaas, Tarjei, *The Ice Palace* (1963), trans. Elizabeth Rokkan (London: Peter Owen, 2005).

Weston, Richard, *Alvar Aalto* (London: Phaidon, 1995).

———, *Säynätsalo Town Hall* (London: Phaidon, 1993).

———, *Utzon: Inspiration, Vision, Architecture* (Copenhagen: Edition Bløndal, 2002).

———, *Villa Mairea* (London: Phaidon, 1992).

Wilson, Colin St John, *Gullichsen/Kairamo/Vormala*, ed. Xavier Güell (Barcelona: Gustavo Gili, 1990).

Wollheim, Richard, ed., *The Image in Form: Selected Writings of Adrian Stokes* (New York: Harper & Row, 1972).

Wrede, Stuart, *The Architecture of Erik Gunnar Asplund* (Cambridge, Massachusetts: MIT Press, 1980).

DIRECTORY OF ARCHITECTS

Numbers in brackets refer to pages on which the architect's work is illustrated

Alvar Aalto, 1898–1976

   [10, 11, 12, 16, 21, 30, 44, 49, 74, 79,

   100, 104, 132, 160, 178, 202, 210, 234]

Klas Anshelm, 1914–80 *[205, 214]*

Gunnar Asplund, 1885–1940 *[72, 77, 81]*

Jean-Jacques Baruël, b. 1923 *[30]*

Jørgen Bo, 1919–99 / Vilhelm Wohlert, 1920–2007 *[96]*

Erik Bryggman, 1891–1955 *[79]*

Molle Cappelen, 1922–86 / Per Cappelen, 1921–78 *[120]*

Peter Celsing, 1920–74 *[18, 229, 236]*

Aarne Ervi, 1910–77 *[74]*

Inger Exner, b. 1926 / Johannes Exner, b. 1926

   [16, 75, 82, 149, 150, 228, 230]

Sverre Fehn, 1924–2009 *[64, 86, 121, 122]*

Kay Fisker, 1893–1965 / C. F. Møller, 1898–1988 /

   Povl Stegmann, 1888–1944 *[48, 148]*

C. F. Hansen, 1756–1845 *[12]*

Arne Jacobsen, 1902–71 *[7, 52, 149, 184, 204, 206]*

Peder Vilhelm Jensen-Klint, 1853–1930 *[180]*

Erkki Kairamo, 1936–94 *[124]*

Sigurd Lewerentz, 1885–1975 *[101, 105, 177, 238]*

Reima Pietilä, 1923–93 *[9, 12, 49, 98, 170]*

Pekka Pitkänen, b. 1927 *[188]*

Aarno Ruusuvuori, 1925–92 *[8, 60, 152, 153, 192, 242]*

Viljo Revell, 1910–64 *[230]*

Kaija Sirén, 1920–2001 / Heikki Sirén, b. 1918 *[136]*

Lars Sonck, 1870–1956 *[176]*

Timo Suomalainen, b. 1928 /

   Tuomo Suomalainen, 1931–88 *[76, 81]*

Jørn Utzon, 1918–2008 *[56, 102]*

Hans van der Laan, 1904–91 *[198]*

3XN *[50, 51]*

   3xn@3xn.dk

   www.3xn.dk

Brunow & Maunula *[47]*

   ark@brunowmaunula.fi

   www.brunowmaunula.fi

Friis & Moltke *[164]*

   mail@friis-moltke.dk

   www.friis-moltke.dk

Terje Grønmo *[151, 196]*

   Østgaard Arkitekter

   post@gronmo.no / post@ostgaard.no

   www.gronmo.no / www.ostgaard.no

Georg Grotenfelt *[231]*

   www.selo.fi

Kristian Gullichsen *[78, 100, 106, 231]*

   architects@gullichsen-vormala.fi

Heikkinen-Komonen Architects *[81, 124]*

   ark@heikkinen-komonen.fi

   www.heikkinen-komonen.fi

Helin & Co *[125]*

   www.helinco.fi

Steven Holl Architects *[34]*

   nyc@stevenholl.com / beijing@stevenholl.com

   www.stevenholl.com

Carl-Viggo Hølmebakk *[102, 126]*

   post@holmebakk.no

   www.holmebakk.no

Järvinen & Airas *[207]*

   Timo Airas

   www.airasarkkitehdit.fi

Järvinen & Nieminen *[140]*

   Kari Järvinen, Merja Nieminen

   www.ark-jn.fi

Jensen & Skodvin *[228]*

   office@jsa.no

   www.jsa.no

JKMM Architects *[144, 148, 179]*

   www.jkmm.fi

Jokela & Kareoja *[110, 224]*

   Olli Pekka Jokela Architects Ltd

   ark@arkopj.fi

   www.arkopj.fi

   Pentti Kareoja, ARK-house Architects

   arkkitehdit@ark-house.com

   www.ark-house.com

Kaira-Lahdelma-Mahlamäki *[123]*

   Mikko Kaira

   mikko.kaira@fcg.fi

KHR Arkitekter *[209]*

   khr@khr.dk / www.khr.dk

Lahdelma & Mahlamäki *[48]*

   Ilmari Lahdelma, Rainer Mahlamäki

   info@arklm.fi

   www.ark-l-m.fi

Henning Larsen Architects *[11, 26, 75, 92, 176, 177,*

   204, 205, 208, 222]

   mail@henninglarsen.com

   www.henninglarsen.com

Juha Leiviskä *[18, 20, 22, 68, 154]*

   www.helander-leiviska.fi

Lund & Slaatto Arkitekter *[116, 246]*

   post@lsa.no

   www.lsa.no

Käpy & Simo Paavilainen *[2, 112, 158, 218]*

   www.ark-paavilainen.fi

PLOT Architects *[46]*

   www.plot.dk

Regnbuen Arkitekter *[36, 40]*

   mail@regnbuen-maa.dk

   www.regnbuen-arkitekter.dk

Matti Sanaksenaho *[128]*

   ark@sanaksenaho.com

   www.kolumbus.fi/sanaksenaho

Arto Sipinen *[19, 123]*

   toimisto@arksipinen.fi

   www.arksipinen.fi

PLACES TO VISIT

Numbers in brackets refer to pages on which the building

is illustrated

Antvorskov Church [36]

Agersøvej 86B, 4200 Slagelse, Denmark

www.antvorskovkirke.dk

Århus Town Hall [7, 52]

Rådhuspladsen 2, 8000 Aarhus, Denmark

www.aarhus.dk

Aukrust Museum [64]

2560 Alvdal, Norway

www.aukrust.no

Bagsværd Church [56]

Taxvej 14–16, 2880 Bagsværd, Denmark

www.bagsvaerdkirke.dk

Benedictine Abbey [198]

Jesu Moder Marias Kloster, Mariavall, 273 95

Tomelilla, Sweden

www.mariavall.se

Chapel of the Holy Cross [188]

Honkaistentie 85, 20900 Turku, Finland

Church of the Good Shepherd [68]

Osoite Palosuontie 1, Pakila, 00660 Helsinki, Finland

http://pakila.helsinginseurakunnat.fi

Copenhagen Business School [26]

Solbjerg Plads 3, 2000 Frederiksberg, Denmark

www.cbs.dk

Dybkær Church [40]

Arendalsvej 1, 8600 Silkeborg, Denmark

www.goedvadsogn.dk

Government Office Building [224]

Aittakarinkatu 21, 26100 Rauma, Finland

Grundtvigs Church [180]

På Bjerget 14B, 2400 Copenhagen, Denmark

http://grundtvigskirke.dk

Gug Church [82, 149]

Nøhr Sørensens Vej 7, 9210 Aalborg, Denmark

www.gugkirke.dk

Hämeenkylä Church [110]

Auratie 3, 01630 Vantaa, Finland

Härlanda Church [236]

Stora Nygatan 1, 411 08 Göteborg, Sweden

Hedmark Museum [86]

Strandvegen 100, 2315 Hamar, Norway

www.hedmarksmuseet.no

Herning Museum of Contemporary Art [34]

Birk Centerpark 8, 7400 Herning, Denmark

www.heartmus.dk

Hospital Chapel [164]

Hobrovej 18–22, 9100 Aalborg, Denmark

www.aalborgsygehus.rn.dk

Huutoniemi Church [242]

Osoite Kuninkaantie 1, 65320 Vaasa, Finland

Hyvinkää Church [60]

Hämeenkatu 16, 05800 Hyvinkää, Finland

IT University of Copenhagen [222]

Rued Langgaards Vej 7, 2300 Copenhagen, Denmark

www.itu.dk

Kaleva Church [98, 170]

Liisanpuisto 1, 33540 Tampere, Finland

Kauniainen Church & Columbarium [78, 106]

Kavallintie 3, 02700 Kauniainen, Finland

Laajasalo Church [140]

Reposalmentie 13, 00840 Helsinki, Finland

Louisiana Museum of Modern Art [96]

Gl. Strandvej 13, 3050 Humlebæk, Denmark

www.louisiana.dk

Malmö Konsthall [214]

Sankt Johannesgatan 7, 211 46 Malmö, Sweden

www.konsthall.malmo.se

Männistö Church [154]

Kellolahdentie 8, 70460 Kuopio, Finland

Myyrmäki Church [22]

Uomatie 1, 01600 Vantaa, Finland

National Bank of Denmark [149, 184]

Havnegade 5, 1093 Copenhagen, Denmark

www.nationalbanken.dk

National Pensions Institute [210]

Nordenskiöldinkatu 12, 00250 Helsinki, Finland

Nordjyllands Art Museum [30]

Kong Christians Allé 50, 9000 Aalborg, Denmark

www.kunsten.dk

Ny Carlsberg Glyptotek Addition [92]

Dantes Plads 7, 1556 Copenhagen, Denmark

www.glyptoteket.dk

Olari Church [2, 218]

Olarinuoma 4, 02200 Espoo, Finland

Pirkkala Church [158]

Suupantie 10, 33960 Pirkkala, Finland

www.pirkkala.seurakunta.net

St Hallvard Church & Abbey [246]

Enerhauggata 4, 0651 Oslo, Norway

http://sthallvard.katolsk.no

St Henry's Chapel [128]

Seiskarinkatu 35, 20900 Turku, Finland

www.henrikin.fi/kappeli

St Magnus Church [116]

Romeriksgata 1, 2003 Lillestrøm, Norway

http://lillestrom.katolsk.no

St Michael Church & Parish Centre [112]

Emännänpolku 1, 00940 Helsinki, Finland

St Peter's Church [238]

Vedbyvägen, 264 35 Klippan, Sweden

Säynätsalo Town Hall [234]

Parviaisentie 9, 40900 Säynätsalo, Finland

www.jyvaskyla.fi/saynatsalo

Student Chapel [136]

Jämeräntaival 8, 02150 Espoo, Finland

Tapiola Church [8, 152, 153, 192]

Kirkkopolku 6, 02100 Espoo, Finland

www.espoonseurakunnat.fi/tapiola

Vardåsen Church [196]

Vardefaret 40, 1388 Borgen, Norway

www.vardasenkirke.no

Viikki Church [144, 148]

Agronominkatu 5, 00790 Helsinki, Finland

Villa Mairea [104, 132]

Noormarkku, Finland

www.villamairea.fi

Vuoksenniska Church [104, 160]

Ruokolahdentie 27, 55800 Imatra, Finland

PICTURE CREDITS

All photographs © Henry Plummer, except for the following: 8 Ordrupgaard, Copenhagen; 13 Ateneum Art Museum, Helsinki; 14 Ateneum Art Museum, Helsinki; 146 Collection of Juhani Pallasmaa; 226 Nasjonalgalleriet, Oslo; 233 Turku Art Museum

Sketches and drawings courtesy of the following: 20 (top and left) Juha Leiviskä; 26 (top) Henning Larsen Architects; 37 (top and below) Regnbuen Arkitekter; 41 (top) Regnbuen Arkitekter; 56 (top and below, left to right) Kim Utzon; 64 (top and below) Sverre Fehn; 66 (top) Juha Leiviskä; 83 (top and left) Inger and Johannes Exner; 91 (top, right) Sverre Fehn; 93 (top and left) Henning Larsen Architects; 106 (top and below) Kristian Gullichsen; 111 (left) Olli-Pekka Jokela; 112 (top) Simo and Käpy Paavilainen; 113 (below) Simo and Käpy Paavilainen; 117 (left, above and below) Kjell Lund; 126 (top and middle row, right) Carl-Viggo Hølmebakk; 129 (top, left and below) Matti Sanaksenaho; 137 (top and right) Kaija and Heikki Sirén; 140 (top, right and below) Järvinen & Nieminen; 144 (top, left to right) JKMM; 154 (top) Juha Leiviskä; 158 (top) Simo and Käpy Paavilainen; 165 (below) Friis & Moltke; 170 (top, above right and right) Raili Pietilä; 196 (top) Terje Grønmo Arkitekter; 219 (top) Simo and Käpy Paavilainen; 224 (right) Olli-Pekka Jokela; 246 (top and right) Kjell Lund.

ACKNOWLEDGMENTS

As this book has evolved over several decades, I am indebted to a great number of people and institutions. First of all I would like to thank Lucas Dietrich at Thames & Hudson, who has given unstinting support and enthusiasm to this project from the outset, and helped to refine its content and scope at an early stage. My gratitude as well to Elain McAlpine, for bringing a critical eye and judicious mind to the book's editing and layout, and to Martin Andersen for a book design so beautifully attuned to Nordic light and architecture.

Providing the crucial financial support for recurring research and photographic visits to Finland, Sweden, Norway and Denmark were the American–Scandinavian Foundation, and on frequent occasions the Campus Research Board, University of Illinois. For their help in writing letters of support to obtain these grants and fellowships, I am most grateful to Jack Baker, Botond Bognar, Mohamed Boubekri, Alejandro Lapunzina, Donlyn Lyndon, Bea Nettles, Juhani Pallasmaa, Richard Peters, Robert Riley and A. Richard Williams. I am thankful as well to David Chasco, director of the School of Architecture, University of Illinois, for lending his wholehearted support to this project and granting a needed sabbatical leave in 2009.

Many architects provided assistance in helping me gain access to their buildings, at times explaining their ideas on site, allowing me to interview them about their treatment of Nordic light, and at a later stage providing architectural drawings. For this I would like to acknowledge my gratitude to Inger and Johannes Exner, Sverre Fehn, Terje Grønmo, Georg Grotenfelt, Kristian Gullichsen, Mikko Heikkinen and Markku Komonen, Pekka Helin, Steven Holl, Carl-Viggo Hølmebakk, Palle Hurwitz of Friis & Moltke, Kari Järvinen, Olli-Pekka Jokela, Henning Larsen, Anssi Lassila, Juha Leiviskä, Lars Lisby and Helge Borup of Regnbuen, Kjell Lund, Samuli Miettinen of JKMM, Simo and Käpy Paavilainen, Juhani Pallasmaa, Raili Pietilä, Anna Ruusuvuori, Matti Sanaksenaho, Arto Sipinen, Kaija and Heikki Sirén, Timo Suomalainen, and Jørn and Kim Utzon. I would also like to convey my appreciation to the countless individuals, too numerous to mention individually, who kindly arranged visits to buildings and were endlessly patient during long and often repeated hours of photography. A special note of thanks goes to Esa Laaksonen, former editor of *Arkkitehti*, for his 1999 publication of a series of my essays on the handling of northern light in Finnish architecture.

It is difficult to give adequate thanks to my longtime friend, Juhani Pallasmaa, for his many subtle contributions to this book. I have benefited from countless discussions with him, over several decades, on the bewitching character of northern light, and its impact not only on Nordic architecture, but also more broadly on its art and culture. He has helped me to better grasp the underlying human and existential concerns of the art of building in this part of the world. Lastly I am at a loss for words in thanking my wife, Patty, who accompanied me on nearly all of the travels underlying this book. It is a blessing to be the repeated beneficiary of someone who can not only cheerfully help with daily practicalities and logistical challenges, making travel a pleasure rather than a burden, but who can also make consistently perceptive and provocative comments on what must often seem an exhausting and endless sequence of buildings. My continuing thanks for this gift.